Also by Philip Ziegler

The Duchess of Dino (1962)

Addington: A Life of Henry Addington, First Viscount Sidmouth (1965)

The Black Death (1969)

King William IV (1971)

Omdurman (1973)

Melbourne: A Biography of William Lamb, 2nd Viscount Melbourne (1976)

Crown and People (1978)

Diana Cooper (1981)

Mountbatten: The Official Biography (1985)

Elizabeth's Britain 1926 to 1986 (1986)

The Diaries of Lord Louis Mountbatten 1920–1922: Tours with the Prince of Wales (1987) (ed.)

Personal Diary of Admiral the Lord Louis Mountbatten, Supreme Allied Commander South-East Asia, 1943–1946 (1988) (ed.)

The Sixth Great Power: Barings 1762–1929 (1988)

From Shore to Shore – The Final Years: The Diaries of Earl Mountbatten of Burma, 1953–1979 (1989) (ed.)

King Edward VIII: The Official Biography (1990)

Brooks's: A Social History (1991) (ed. with Desmond Seward)

Wilson: The Authorised Life of Lord Wilson of Rievaulx (1993)

London at War 1939–1945 (1995)

Osbert Sitwell (1998)

Britain Then and Now: The Francis Frith Collection (1999)

Soldiers: Fighting Men's Lives, 1901–2001 (2001)

Man Of Letters: The Extraordinary Life and Times of Literary Impresario Rupert Hart-Davis (2005)

Edward Heath: The Authorised Biography (2010)

Olivier (2013)

George VI: The Dutiful King (2014)

Philip Ziegler

BETWEEN THE WARS
1919–1939

MACLEHOSE PRESS
QUERCUS · LONDON

First published in Great Britain in 2016 by MacLehose Press
This paperback edition published in 2017 by

MacLehose Press
An imprint of Quercus Publishing Ltd
Carmelite House
50 Victoria Embankment
London EC4Y 0DZ

An Hachette UK company

A CIP catalogue record for this book is available
from the British Library

ISBN (MMP) 978 0 85705 523 1
ISBN (Ebook) 978 0 85705 524 8

2 4 6 8 10 9 7 5 3 1

CONTENTS

PROLOGUE

People do not often know a great deal about the decades immediately before and after they were born; the first is too late to be history, the second too early. I was born in 1929. The inter-war years, between 1919 and 1939, are therefore relatively unknown to me. In the course of my life I have, of course, read many books written during or about that period, but my knowledge was far less systematic than was true, say, of the years before 1914 or after 1945. I resolved to put that right.

This book is, therefore, a voyage of discovery. It is not a book for specialists; with the exception of the abdication crisis, there is no subject about which those who are authorities in their respective fields do not know far more than I do. I have relied on the work of these experts, am most grateful to them for their labours and hope that I have not misused or misrepresented their scholarship.

The choice of subjects is arbitrary and reflects my own tastes and interests. I have, for instance, devoted a chapter to the publication of James Joyce's *Ulysses*. It might as well have been E. M. Forster's *A Passage to India*, Hemingway's *A Farewell to Arms*, Kafka's *The Castle* or Sartre's *Nausea*. There can be no right or wrong in such matters: all these are great novels, the choice of any one of them could be justified convincingly. I have sought to touch on all parts of the world and all the main fields of human endeavour. I have failed. There is, for instance, no chapter on Australasia. To suggest that nothing of importance happened in Australia or New Zealand between 1919 and 1939 would be as silly as it would be impertinent: it just happened that there was no convenient peg on which to hang a chapter at a time at which something of greater moment was not going on elsewhere. Any readers of this book are likely to ask themselves: "Why on earth did he include this?" or "How can he possibly have omitted that?" They will be fully justified in doing so. There are many more or less significant incidents in world history that this book might have covered, but my primary concern has been to follow what emerged as the two main themes: the recession of European power and the road to the Second World War. These have in large part determined the choices that I have made.

All I can say with confidence is that the book has been most enjoyable to write. I hope that it will be equally enjoyable to read.

1

PEACE

1919–20

In Paris, in the first six months of 1919, a group of intelligent, experi-
enced and well-intentioned men were busily preparing the ground
for the next World War. This was, of course, the very opposite of their
intentions. Europe was just emerging from more than four years
of disastrous and hideously destructive conflict. Nearly two million
Germans had died in the fighting, almost as many Russians, well over
a million French and Austro-Hungarians, three-quarters of a mil-
lion British with another two hundred thousand from the Empire.
Italy had been scarred by the fighting; vast tracts of France and Bel-
gium devastated. If there was one thing that the negotiators took for
granted it was that it must never happen again. This had to have
been the war to end wars.

* * *

In the eyes of the victorious Allies at least, it was unequivocally
Germany which had been responsible for the First World War.
Their prime consideration was that this should never be allowed
to happen again. There were, of course, many other issues which
would have to be regulated before the world could begin to recover from the carnage of war, but in the eyes of the participants

Lloyd George, Clemenceau and Woodrow Wilson stroll, rather self-consciously, down the Champs-Élysées during the Peace Conference of 1919.

the future of Germany was their first preoccupation. The subsidiary problems, it was fondly assumed, would quickly be disposed of. Even where Germany was concerned the negotiators saw no reason to believe that there would be serious disagreement. At the end of 1918 Raymond Poincaré, the French President, told an American journalist that he did not expect the Peace Conference would have the least trouble in arriving at complete agreement: "All the principles were already in harmony and the general lines and details would be settled as soon as the delegates got to work." The remarkable thing about this observation is that Poincaré was not merely mouthing pious platitudes for the benefit of the press but actually believed that what he said was true. Still more remarkable is that his fellow delegates, even if they had certain minor reservations, should have shared his optimism.

The first problem, of course, was to decide who those fellow delegates should be. It was not just a question of settling the frontiers of Germany and deciding what reparations should be extracted from the defeated enemy: the future of many other nations was in the melting pot. To the Poles, the Romanians, the Yugoslavs, the Bulgarians, the Czechs, the Slovaks, the Hungarians, the Greeks, the treatment of Germany was a matter for concern certainly, but a peripheral consideration when compared with the question of their own independent existences. And then there were the Turks, the Arabs, the Japanese: if every nationality whose interests were involved had been given equal opportunity to voice their views at the Conference, no hall would have been large enough to accommodate them, no debate long enough to provide time for all their speeches. When Roman Dmowski, head of the Polish National Committee in Paris, was given a chance to expatiate on the woes of his country, he began, complained an American delegate, "at eleven o'clock in the morning and could reach 1919 and the pressing problems of the moment only as late as four o'clock in the afternoon. Edvard Beneš for Czechoslovakia began a century earlier and finished an hour later".

Clearly, if anything were to be achieved, it would have to be in a smaller forum. On 12 January, 1919, the political leaders of Britain, France, Italy and the United States, accompanied by their foreign secretaries, met at the Quai d'Orsay, the French foreign office on the banks of the Seine. On the insistence of the British, the Japanese were then invited to join the inner group, creating the Council of Ten or Supreme Council. This also proved too cumbersome: the Japanese – on the somewhat flimsy grounds that they were not represented by their Prime Minister – were dropped as abruptly as they had been taken up. Foreign secretaries, too, were decided to be superfluous. The Council of Ten gave way to the Council of Four – Britain, France, Italy and the United States. Even this was not the end. Vittorio Orlando, the Italian Prime Minister, took little interest in anything that did not directly relate to his own country and, anyway, was so preoccupied by his precarious political standing in Italy that he missed as many meetings as he attended. The Big Four became, *de facto*, the Big Three. The future of Europe, indeed to a large extent, the future of the world was in their hands. The fact that two of the three countries were English-speaking led to a change in the way that the world's affairs were managed. Until 1919 French had been the traditional language of diplomacy; now, to the indignation of the host-nation, the Americans and

British insisted that English should rank with French as being the official language of the Conference.

* * *

Two prime ministers and a president: each, of course, representing the interests of his own country yet also three individuals with very much their own personalities and points of view who were capable on occasion of acting with striking disregard for their national advisers or the demands of their own domestic politics. By far the oldest and in some ways the most formidable was the French premier, Georges Clemenceau. Once his President, Raimond Poincaré, whom Clemenceau disliked and despised, had formally opened the Conference, the premier took matters into his own hands, almost completely ignoring his affable but lightweight Foreign Minister, Stéphen Pichon. He was fiercely patriotic and jealous in defence of anything which he saw as being in the national interest. He spoke English far better than his British and American colleagues spoke French but he would not for a moment have contemplated using any language other than French when discussions were officially in progress. Most of his life had been spent in politics and by instinct he was radical and anti-clerical; but he was not over-concerned with philosophical issues. His aim always was to get the best deal for France: if that conflicted with some abstract principle then so much the worse for the principle. His method of conducting a meeting was autocratic: when somebody had propounded a view which corresponded with his own he would glare round the room. "*Y a-t-il d'objections?*" he would demand, then, before any opposition had

had a chance to voice itself: *"Non? Adopté!"* "I must say Clemenceau is extremely rude to the small Powers," noted the young British diplomat, Harold Nicolson, "but then he is extremely rude to the big Powers also." His nickname was "The Tiger" and like a tiger he preferred to hunt alone, killed with speed and efficiency and guarded his prey with singular ferocity. He rejoiced in doing his own thing with scant regard for the cherished conventions and formalities of other people. After the official opening of the Conference he found himself walking down the steps with the British Foreign Secretary, Arthur Balfour. Balfour was wearing a top hat, Clemenceau a bowler. Balfour apologised for his apparent solecism: "I was told," he explained, "that it was obligatory to wear a top hat." *"Moi aussi,"* said Clemenceau.

Though Balfour was by instinct discreet and conformist his own Prime Minister would have been as likely as Clemenceau to defy convention. David Lloyd George was a Welshman and he displayed all the sensibility, the eloquence and the volatility traditionally associated with that wayward breed. He was a left-wing liberal, a radical from the lower middle classes in charge of an administration that was predominantly conservative and dominated by the landed gentry. His position was therefore precarious, a consideration which rarely affected his course of action. His main problem as a negotiator was that his fellow statesmen did not altogether trust him: they believed that he was erratic and inconsistent; quick to change his opinion if he saw tactical advantage in so doing; at times intoxicated by his own eloquence; a man of few principles and by no means committed even to those principles that he had. In this they were unfair, but not without some grounds for their opinion. It was easy to admire

Lloyd George, even to love him, but it was difficult to put complete faith in his integrity or the coherence of his views.

Clemenceau and Lloyd George were very different animals; they surveyed each other with perplexed surmise, wondering what the other was going on about and what he might do next. Compared, however, with the American President, Woodrow Wilson, they were recognisably creatures of a similar species who found themselves confronted by an alien, if not from outer space then at least from a different world. Wilson was that admirable if slightly alarming phenomenon, an idealistic politician. He was also an American: a circumstance which perhaps made it easier for him to retain his ideals unblemished but also inspired a sense, if not of inferiority, then at least self-doubt when confronted by the wily and world-weary Europeans. He came across the Atlantic as a Messiah resolved to sweep the professional politicians out of the temple and impose new standards of honour and integrity. Yet he came also as a timid debutant, aware that he had little experience of international affairs and anxious not to expose his ignorance or in any way make a fool of himself. Balfour was impressed by him and surprised to find him as competent round a conference table as he was on paper: "His attitude at the meetings of the Big Four is firm, modest, restrained, eloquent, well informed and convincing . . ." And yet at the same time the Europeans found him a little ridiculous, inclined to sanctimony, self-important, overwhelmed by the conviction of his own rectitude. He came armed with his precious Fourteen Points, on the basis of which he believed negotiations should be conducted. "God himself was content with ten commandments," complained Clemenceau. "Wilson modestly inflicted fourteen points on us . . . fourteen commandments of . . . empty theory."

The most pertinent of Wilson's Points, so far as the negotiators were concerned, related to self-determination: no population, he believed, should be subjected against its will to foreign rule. The principle was patently admirable; the problems started when one tried to define what constituted a population and when its rulers should be deemed foreign. Wilson's task was all the harder in that he was trying to impose his vision on a world which was already bound by a plethora of private deals that had been struck long before the Americans with their idealistic baggage had appeared on the scene. Italy, for instance, considered that it had already been promised territories currently inhabited by Greeks, Slavs, Germans and Albanians; Romania, territories inhabited by Hungarians; in the Middle East it was understood that France was to take over lands which the Arabs felt should rightly be under their governance; in Africa Great Britain took it for granted that the bulk of the former German colonies should be added to its own Empire. Were all such arrangements to be swept aside to accommodate President Wilson's prejudices? Not if the Italians, French and British were to have anything to do with it. From the moment that the Conference opened it was clear that the participants were not merely pursuing different objectives but were advancing along paths so divergent that it seemed all too possible that they might never meet.

* * *

The Conference should never have had its seat in France. The original plan had been to hold it in a neutral country, probably

Switzerland, but Clemenceau argued that peace should be made in the country that had borne the brunt of the fighting. "I never wanted to hold the Conference in his bloody capital!" Lloyd George complained, but, he claimed, he had allowed himself to be overborne by the old man's protestations. In fact it seems that Clemenceau himself had been overborne and had resigned himself to a Conference held outside France. It was only when the Americans got cold feet about the security available for their President in a neutral country that France was accepted as the venue. "Switzerland," Wilson declared, basing his view on information which he presumably found convincing but does not seem to have been available to any other participant, "was saturated with every kind of poisonous element." The French were delighted to accept the accuracy of this revelation; the British were doubtful but did not care that much; Paris it was.

The result was that the Conference took place in the capital of a country which had been ravaged by war and whose population was possessed by an urge to wreak vengeance on those who they deemed to have been been responsible for their sufferings. One cannot tell whether, if the meetings had taken place in a neutral country, the deliberations would have been more dispassionate or the conclusions more balanced, but the rancorous mood of the Parisian population must to some extent have penetrated the walls of the Quai d'Orsay and coloured the mood of the chief negotiators.

It was not because of that, however, that what could have been, perhaps *should* have been, the most important by-product of the Conference was never allowed to realise its full potential. Woodrow Wilson arrived in Paris armed not merely with his

Fourteen Points but also with the blueprint for an organisation that he believed could transform the world. The League of Nations, as he conceived it, would have had as its members every independent country in the world. It would have wielded an authority, legal as well as moral, far more mighty than that enjoyed by any of its constituent parts. Wilson's League would have provided a forum in which any international dispute could be discussed and resolved. It would have made war inconceivable if not impossible. The French were sceptical: in principle they quite liked the idea, but Clemenceau would never have contemplated any significant sacrifice of national sovereignty unless he had first been very sure that French interests would be protected. The British were sceptical: the League would be no substitute for the British Fleet, said Winston Churchill. Even the Americans were sceptical: Senator Henry Cabot Lodge believed that Wilson was prepared to sacrifice the independence of the United States not in the interests of world government but to fuel his own insensate lust for glory. Only Woodrow Wilson unequivocally believed, yet so great was his prestige, so spectacular had been his welcome when he arrived in Europe, that it seemed for a time as if his dream might come true.

So, up to a point, it did. The League of Nations took off, but, tragically, Wilson, when pursuing his dream in Europe, had failed to fortify his power base at home. Lodge proposed various reservations on American membership of the League which would have reduced its potential role to the level of futility. Wilson rejected them all and went on a crusade around the United States, preaching the merits of a powerful and truly all-inclusive League. He may have convinced the American man in the street, but when the entry of the United States into the League of Nations was debated in the Senate he failed to obtain the necessary two-thirds majority. Wilson, already a sick man, died a few years later; the League of Nations, without American participation, limped along, doing some useful work but notably failing to provide the strong international presence that, a few years later, might have made the bellicose adventures of Germany and Italy much more difficult, if not prevented them altogether.

There remained the task for which the Conference had primarily been set up: the reshaping of Europe from the ravaged ruins which five years of war had left behind. The two great entities that had dominated Central and Eastern Europe during the nineteenth century – the Ottoman and the Austro-Hungarian Empires – had crumbled into ruins. The age of the nation state had dawned – but which were the nations and how were their boundaries to be drawn? Poland, for one, clearly had to be given frontiers that would enable it to establish a viable country, but this could only be done at the expense of other claimants. In the east it would involve the incorporation of territories that Russia considered to be traditionally its own. Russia was in chaos and, in the short term, could safely be ignored, but in the interests of the long-term stability of Europe it was obviously desirable not to establish frontiers that would seem unacceptable to whatever government finally established itself in Moscow. The same was true in the west. In this case it was the Germans who would lose out territorially. Nobody, in early 1919, was disposed to pay much attention to German protestations, but by the time that the frontiers between Poland and Germany were eventually established in 1922 Germany had to a great extent been accepted back into the comity of nations. Nevertheless, in territorial terms, it was the clear loser. The result satisfied nobody: which up to a point suggested that it was fair and reasonable but left a substantial German minority under Polish rule. It was an uneasy compromise that carried within itself the seeds of its own destruction. Of all the conclusions reached at Versailles, it pointed the most inexorably towards September 1939.

And then there were the Czechs. Edvard Beneš, Shadow Foreign Minister in the putative government of an independent Czechoslovakia, was one of the most eloquent and persuasive of those delegates who pleaded for a homeland that would be politically homogeneous and economically viable. In this case there were, of course, two ethnic groups which had to be accommodated, but at the end of the First World War it seemed that Czechs and Slovaks were ready to make common cause in the building of a new nation. More significantly, however, there were three million Sudeten Germans who would willy-nilly be included in what was becoming Czechoslovakia. Like their counterparts in the new Poland, they were not in a position to make much of a fuss about their incorporation in this alien nation but they remained an ill-digested fragment of what was anyway a fissiparous community. It was painfully analogous to the situation in Poland. The negotiators at Versailles assured themselves that they were building a stable continent yet they were instead creating the conditions that would almost inevitably lead to increasing instability and eventual war.

Yugoslavia, Bulgaria, Hungary: there seemed to be no country in Eastern Europe that, in the opinion of its inhabitants, was within its proper frontiers or could boast a population that was politically or ethnically united. The lines of partition were arbitrary, drawn on a map by men who knew little of the human beings of whom they were so summarily disposing but who knew too that no amount of research and agonising could produce a result that would be satisfactory to everybody. What made the situation more complicated was that they suspected – and in all probability suspected rightly – that delay could only make things worse.

* * *

It was not in Europe alone that the negotiators were creating a new world. The collapse of the Ottoman Empire meant that the Middle East was largely a blank canvas in urgent need of filling in. Any illusions the Americans might have cherished that this process could be conducted with calm objectivity and without undue regard to previous commitments were rapidly dispelled. "It is appalling that these ignorant and irresponsible men should be cutting Asia Minor to bits as if they were dividing a cake," Harold Nicolson wrote indignantly to his wife. "Isn't it terrible, the happiness of millions being decided in that way?" Irresponsible, perhaps, but the French and British were far from ignorant. On the contrary, for generations they had been active in that area, carving out zones in which they felt themselves pre-eminent and selecting those among the Arab leaders whom they felt could safely be relied on to act, if not as puppets, then at least as safe and reasonably docile friends. The rapid growth of oil production in the area lent a new significance to these manoeuvres. Mark Sykes and François Georges-Picot had done a deal in 1916, under the aegis of the British and French governments and with the silent agreement of Russia, which more or less partitioned the Middle East into zones of British or French supremacy. By the end of 1918 things had changed little in essentials. Both sides were vaguely discontented with their share of the loot; but that it *was* loot, that it was *their* loot, and that there was little room for American interference, was common ground. The Americans were a fact of life, however, and could not be ignored, especially with Wilson propagating extravagant ideas of independence among the Arab leaders. The best course, the French and British concluded, would be to make some *apparent* concessions to Arab nationalism; the Arab nationals concerned, however, being hand-picked to ensure that they would champion the cause of their sponsoring great power. The favoured British candidate for an "independent" Arab leader was the man who would become King Faisal: engaging, ambitious, courageous and a descendant of the Prophet, with that most evasive hero, the mysterious and magnetically attractive Lawrence of Arabia, always at his side. To what extent Faisal should enjoy real independence, what areas should remain under British or French mandate, whether the United States should also enjoy a mandated area, what the term "mandate" actually meant, were all issues that were discussed at great length at Versailles. Little was reached by way of con-clusions, and it was well into the 1920s before the Middle East achieved any semblance of stability.

The development which, above all others, was to endanger that stability had occurred long before the Treaty of Versailles. It was in October 1917 that Balfour had told Lord Rothschild that the British government was committed to establishing a national home for the Jewish people in Palestine.

"National home" did not mean "nation", he insisted: a distinction that the Jewish leader, Chaim Weizmann, professed to accept, though he could have had little doubt that the state of Israel would be a political fact before many years had passed. Many Jews were dubious about the proposition: they saw themselves as loyally British, French or German and deplored a development that would to some extent distinguish them from their fellow citizens. Some Gentiles had doubts on other grounds. What, they wondered, was to become of the unfortunate Arabs whose homeland was to be thus invaded? Would they be displaced? Could they be expected to co-exist peacefully with their new neighbours? To Weizmann and the other ardent Zionists such doubts were insignificant compared with the transcendent glory of a Jewish homeland. Two thousand years of victimisation would be at an end: those Arabs who were too short-sighted to see that their future would be far brighter in an efficiently run and politically stable Jewish state must be cajoled or coerced into acquiescence. If the worst came to the worst, they would have to be ignored.

By the time that Weizmann and his colleagues made their way to Versailles in January 1919 the main issues about the Jewish homeland had tacitly or explicitly been settled. What remained to be decided were the exact frontiers of the new state and who should police an operation that was likely to be hotly contested during the first few years at least. Weizmann was not particularly concerned about whatever Arab opposition to the Jewish state might be voiced at Versailles. He knew that he was far more articulate and eloquent than anyone who might argue the Arab cause and, anyway, the Arabs had as yet hardly begun to take in what was going on, let alone to organise effective opposition. He was more conscious of the danger from his own side, from those Jews who thought that the whole idea of a homeland was ill-conceived and dangerous. On the whole, though, he felt confident that all would go well. He was proved right. Very little of significance about the Jewish homeland was actually decided at Versailles, but the fact that its existence was taken for granted was of immeasurable importance. By the time that the Conference had ended, for better or for worse, the future Israel had become a fact of life.

* * *

It is above all by their treatment of the defeated foe that the negotiators at Versailles are remembered. The conventional rendering of events is attractively straightforward: Britain and the United States were inclined to be magnanimous, but the vengeful French insisted on terms so harsh, both territorial and financial, that their acceptance by the Germans could never be more than resentfully half-hearted. The Treaty of Versailles thus prepared the way for the rise of Fascism and the Second World War. Like all generalisations this is a gross over-simplification and needs to be infinitely qualified; like most generalisations it contains a disconcerting measure of truth.

That the French were vengeful and that they had some right to be so can hardly be disputed. What is more to the point is that they were afraid. Twice within fifty years their country had been overrun by a victorious enemy from the east; their prime consideration was that this should not be allowed to happen again. The best way of ensuring this, they concluded, perhaps the only way of ensuring this, was by reducing Germany to a condition where politically, economically and militarily it would never have the strength to challenge France again. Fear was the main driving force behind the French policy at Versailles. The fact that they also hated the Germans added piquancy to their quest for permanent supremacy but did not fundamentally shape it. It was still a potent and omnipresent factor, however. Inevitably, the animosity dwindled as memories of the war grew more distant, but for the first year or two after the end of hostilities the French viewed the Germans as almost subhuman, not fit to be treated as full members of the human race. In the spring of 1919 an English lady went into a chemist's shop in Versailles and asked if they had any aspirin. For some reason the chemist took it that she was the wife of one the German delegates who had recently arrived in town. "We have, but not for you!" he replied proudly. For a French shopkeeper to renounce the opportunity for a sale argued a formidable degree of animosity. The French negotiators were somewhat more sophisticated, but the underlying sentiment was much the same.

There were three main issues to be resolved: the boundaries of post-war Germany, the measures to be taken to ensure that German militarism was never revived and the degree to which Germany should be required to reimburse the victors for the financial losses that they had suffered during the war. The settlement of Germany's frontiers provided the first evidence that the Conference was not going to be as uncontroversial as Poincaré had supposed. As far as the north, south and east were concerned the shape of the new Germany, however disastrous the conclusions of the Conference turned out to be, led to relatively little debate; it was in the west that the serious problems arose. In the eyes of the French the Rhine was the natural frontier between France and Germany. Geographically this made sense. Unfortunately, however, there existed to the west of the Rhine a large, densely populated and heavily industrialised province the population of which was almost entirely German-speaking. They were French at heart, Clemenceau contended optimistically; unfortunately he could find scant evidence to support his claim. The Rhinelanders showed little enthusiasm for setting up an independent state and still less for becoming part of France. Left to themselves the Americans and British would probably have favoured keeping the Rhineland in Germany, perhaps under some kind of temporary international mandate. The French protested furiously. By April 1919 the debate had become so embittered that Lloyd George and Wilson both retired to their beds and Wilson ordered a battleship, the *George Washington*, to be available to take him back to the United States. Eventually a compromise emerged. The main French fear was that the Rhineland would provide a base west of the Rhine where Germany could build up its forces preparatory to an attack on France. The area, therefore, should be permanently demilitarised, and be occupied for an unspecified number of years by Allied troops. For this to work in the long term the continued acquiescence of Germany would be required; in 1919 it did not seem too much to hope that this would be forthcoming.

* * *

Even though it might not be able to launch an assault on France from the Rhineland, the spectre of a rearmed Germany bent on revenge filled the French government and people with an apprehension that was perhaps exaggerated but could not be dismissed as wholly unreasonable. The French government's preferred solution was that not merely the Rhineland but all of Germany should be demilitarised, and not just for a few years but for ever. The more reasonable members of their government privately admitted that, in international politics, there could be no such concept as "for ever", but something close to it was still their aim. Britain and the United States were not altogether unsympathetic but a new and alarming factor now influenced their thinking. The revolution that had convulsed Russia had led to the almost complete triumph of Bolshevism. Russia was still in the process of rebuilding itself after the carnage of the war and revolution but already it was showing its resolve to foment the spread of Communism in the countries to its west. Germany, with its economy shattered by defeat and its political structure largely dismantled, was an obvious and tempting target. If it was totally deprived of armed forces it would be unable to combat any threat, internal or external, that Communism might pose. Something larger than a police force but smaller than an army seemed the solution. The French rather grudgingly agreed; the German government, which would have viewed with horror any suggestion that their country should even be contemplating the possibility of engaging in a new conflict, were happy to accept the proposition; those Germans who dreamed of rearmament and revenge were comforted by the notion that a structure would exist which could be quickly built on and expanded when an opportunity occurred.

* * *

It was the question of reparations that did most to undermine the unity of the victors and create lasting rancour among the defeated. Broadly speaking – and only the broadest speaking could save both author and reader from being lost in a jungle of statistics – there were two schools of thought. The more vengeful, led, inevitably by the French, held that Germany should make good all, or at least the greater part, of the costs of the First World War – including the expenses of the Allied war effort on top of the damage inflicted on civilians, mainly in France and Belgium. If taken literally this would have imposed on Germany a burden so overwhelming that recovery could never have been achieved; the French would not have pushed things quite to such a point, but in their view the protracted suffering of the German people was almost as important an element of any settlement as was the provision of compensation for their victims. The view championed by the Americans, on the other hand, was that the Germans should be required only to make good the damage inflicted on the civilian populations of the countries that they had bombed or overrun. This was onerous enough but something that could be reconciled with, indeed in the long term depended on, Germany's economic recovery. The British were somewhere between the two. Lloyd George affected to strike a benevolent note. "We must offer terms," he insisted, "which a responsible government in Germany can expect to carry out." The period during which Germany should be expected to pay reparations should not be protracted beyond the lifetime of the generation which had made the war. When it came to deciding the actual figures, though, he proved to be little if at all more liberal than

Clemenceau. The Americans would have been more generous, but, as the partner who had suffered least, they hesitated to impose their views upon their allies. The proceedings of the Reparations Commission were intolerably protracted – Lord Sumner, a judge who formed part of the British delegation, remarked that they seemed likely to last not merely until the signing of the treaties of peace but even until the outbreak of the next war – but in the end figures were agreed.

They fully satisfied no-one, but they appalled the Germans. That millions of German speakers should be placed under foreign rule was distressing, but that did not actually affect the daily lives of the much greater number who lived outside the affected areas. Reparations, on the other hand, would lay a crippling burden on the shoulders of every man, woman and child, a burden that would have to be borne for many years, almost, it seemed, in perpetuity. The Germans accepted the terms; they had no option. "We commend our unhappy country to the care of a merciful God," said the Chairman of the German National Assembly at the end of the debate that preceded acceptance. At least, he must have thought, God could hardly be less merciful than the victorious allies.

There were many among those allies who felt that a dreadful mistake had been made. Harold Nicolson was standing near Clemenceau when someone congratulated the veteran statesman on this glorious conclusion. "*Oui,*" Clemenceau said, "*c'est une belle journée.*" Nicolson turned to his neighbour, Madame Murat. "'*En êtes vous sur?*' I ask her. '*Pas du tout,*' she answers, being a woman of intelligence." "Immoral and senseless," Nicolson described the final figures. "There is not a single person among the younger people here who is not unhappy and disappointed with the terms." It was not only the younger people who were sceptical. Jan Smuts told Lloyd George that the Treaty breathed "a poisonous spirit of revenge, which may yet scorch the fair face – not of a corner of France, but of Europe". "This is not peace," Marshal Foch is said to have remarked presciently. "It is an Armistice for twenty years."

As Margaret Macmillan has argued in her admirable study of the episode, *Peacemakers*, it is not fair to blame what happened over those next twenty years exclusively, or even primarily on the Treaty of Versailles. If the Americans had not largely lost interest in Europe, if the British and French governments had been more resolute in enforcing the terms of the Treaty, if the economic depression had not undermined the democratic government of Germany, then things could have been very different. But the terms of the Treaty created the conditions which would inevitably lead in due course to a German wish to reverse them and yet did not so emasculate Germany as to render it forever unable to muster the strength to achieve its end. The Treaty of Versailles did not directly cause the Second World War, but if the Treaty had been drafted with greater realism and foresight, the Second World War might never have occurred.

NOTES FOR FURTHER READING

Margaret MacMillan's *Peacemakers* (London 2001) provides the best overall picture of the negotiations at the end of the First World War though it does not wholly replace F. S. Marston's *The Versailles Settlement* (London 1991). Among the many relevant biographies are David Gilmour's *Curzon* (London 1994), Gregor Dallas's *At the Heart of a Tiger: Clemenceau and His World* (London 1993) and A. Scott Berg's *Woodrow Wilson* (New York 2013). John Grigg, alas, did not live to finish his majestic biography of Lloyd George, but Roy Hattersley's *David Lloyd George. The Great Outsider* (London 2010) is very readable.

2

HOME RULE FOR IRELAND

1921

Number Ten, Downing Street: 2.20 in the morning of Tuesday, 6 December, 1921. The final meeting had begun three hours before, but the negotiations that had led up to it had been going on for two months or more. At last, it was all over. After some 750 years of rule from London the Irish had gained their independence.

* * *

It had been a long and often blood-stained path that had led to its end on that day in Downing Street. Though there had been periods of relative tranquility Ireland had never accepted its assimilation into the United Kingdom. Successive independence movements had been crushed by brutal military repression or, as the English saw it, successive disturbances fomented by a vicious and unrepresentative minority had been quelled in the interests of law and order. In London's view the Act of Union of 1800 had settled the matter for ever; to a majority of those in Dublin it seemed that union imposed by the English without any pretence of consultation with the Irish people had merely added fresh insult to an already intolerable injury. Nearly a century of dissension followed before Gladstone concluded that both justice and

THE ILLUSTRATED LONDON NEWS

REGISTERED AS A NEWSPAPER FOR TRANSMISSION IN THE UNITED KINGDOM AND TO CANADA AND NEWFOUNDLAND BY MAGAZINE POST.

SATURDAY, JULY 23, 1921.

The Copyright of all the Editorial Matter, both Engravings and Letterpress, is Strictly Reserved in Great Britain, the Colonies, Europe, and the United States of America.

MAKING IRISH HISTORY AT 10, DOWNING STREET: MR. LLOYD GEORGE AND MR. DE VALERA MEET ALONE, TO DISCUSS PEACE.

The first meeting between Mr. Lloyd George and Mr. de Valera took place in the drawing-room at the Premier's official residence, No. 10, Downing Street, on July 14. The official statement issued afterwards said : " Mr. Lloyd George and Mr. de Valera met as arranged at 4.30 p.m. at 10, Downing Street. They were alone, and the conversation lasted until 7 p.m. A full exchange of views took place, and relative positions were defined." Other important conferences have followed. Sir James Craig has returned to Belfast, leaving Mr. Lloyd George and Mr. de Valera to work out their own solution for the South.

DRAWN BY OUR SPECIAL ARTIST, STEVEN SPURRIER. COPYRIGHTED IN THE UNITED STATES AND CANADA.

De Valera and Lloyd George in Downing Street in July 1921 shortly
before the signature of the Treaty of London.

self-interest demanded that the boil should be lanced. His Home Rule Bill of 1886, though it was greeted with outrage by the Conservatives and stirred up many doubts among his own followers, was a modest measure which could never in the long run have satisfied the ambitions of the Irish nationalists. At the time, however, it seemed a momentous and probably even an irrevocable step.

It raised as many questions as it answered. What was "Rule"? Was it true independence that was being offered to the Irish? A foreign policy distinct from that of the rest of Britain? Responsibility for its own defence? And, still more pertinently, what was "Home"? It was this last that caused the bitterest dissension. In the greater part of Ireland the majority of the population was indigenous and Roman Catholic; in Ulster to the north-east, however, there had over the centuries been substantial immigration from Scotland and more than half the inhabitants were not merely Protestant but fiercely Presbyterian. The question of how these people would fit into a predominantly Catholic and independent Ireland had not at first preoccupied those Englishmen who accepted responsibility for Ireland's future. Since Catholic Emancipation in 1829 the Roman Catholics in England seemed to have got along without too much bother; no doubt the same would be true of the Protestants in Ireland. Such complacency did not long survive the introduction of Gladstone's Home Rule Bill. It had been accepted that some filibustering was inevitable – the inhabitants of Ulster could never have been expected to welcome their absorption into an independent Ireland – but nobody thought that it would amount to much or last for long. Conceivably this could have proved to be the case if the doubts of the Northern Irish had not been articulated and trumpeted abroad by the maverick Conservative, Randolph Churchill. "Ulster will fight and Ulster will be right!" he proclaimed, and under this intransigent banner the Protestants of the North prepared to protect their patrimony.

The need for such a defence did not seem particularly pressing. The House of Lords proved to be almost as intransigent as the Ulster Protestants and struck down with indecent relish any legislation that the Lower House might introduce to reform the Irish constitution. It was more than twenty years after Gladstone's initiative before the Parliament Act of 1911 curbed the power of the Lords and made it possible for a measure envisaging a substantial degree of Irish independence to become law. By then the forces of opposition had mustered. Edward Carson, the new leader of the Ulster Unionists, was to the fore. "We must be prepared," he proclaimed in September 1911, "the morning Home Rule passes, ourselves to become responsible for the government of the Protestant Province of Ulster." The possibility that patriotic Protestants, intent only on remaining British, should be coerced by British arms into accepting the alien rule of Catholic Ireland, was patently unacceptable to a large part of the population; it even seemed uncertain whether British troops would obey orders if they were told to enforce such a ruling by crushing Protestant opposition in the North. Finally it was accepted by all parties in London that some sort of partition must be imposed, but what the frontiers should be and how absolute would be the degree of severance were issues that seemed almost impossible to resolve. The outbreak of the First World War in July 1914 had at least one glimmer of a silver lining;

that the fate of Ireland could be put on the back burner until this more urgent business had been settled.

John Redmond, the moderate leader of the Irish nationalists, was well content that this should be so. He urged his followers to join in the battle against Germany, believing that, if the Catholics of the South fought side by side with the Protestants of the North, then all thoughts of partition would be put aside. For a time it seemed that his belief might be borne out by events; though Sinn Féin, the party committed to a wholly independent Ireland and the rejection of any link with the rest of Britain, was growing in strength, it was still relatively inconsiderable when the war broke out. Redmond thought he could afford to ignore or at least pay little attention to it. When the more extreme Irish nationalists rose over Easter 1916 and temporarily took control of Dublin, Redmond denounced them. His position was undermined, however, when the British, having crushed the Easter Rising, ignored his appeals for clemency and proceeded to execute many of the captured leaders. This ruthlessness forfeited the sympathy of the Irish moderates, yet at the same time spared some of those leaders, including Michael Collins and Eámon de Valera, two revolutionary leaders who were to be among the most prominent in the battles for independence that lay ahead. The British government again played into the republicans' hands by its misguided attempt to impose conscription on Ireland in April 1918; the threat achieved nothing except the alienation, once again, of many moderate Irishmen. By then Redmond was dead; in the election at the end of the year Sinn Féin swept the board and became unequivocally the majority party in whatever government was to rule in Ireland.

There followed some two years of messy semi-war: not a war with battle-lines in which clear-cut victories and defeats were possible but a vicious and murderous campaign in which the irregulars on both sides bore the brunt of the fighting and committed the worst of the atrocities. If there was one man more than any other who deserves the credit for realising that this must stop, it was the British Prime Minister, David Lloyd George. As in Paris two years before, Lloyd George's freedom of action was circumscribed by the fact that he, a radical, was leading a government which was predominantly Conservative; as in Paris he managed largely to overcome that handicap and conduct a strikingly individual policy. Lloyd George wanted to talk to Michael Collins: "No doubt he is the head and font of the movement. If I could see him a settlement might be possible." But would the British people, most particularly the Conservatives upon whose support he depended, be ready to agree that he should negotiate with people whom they had been taught to think of as murderous rebels? As a preliminary step, at the end of 1920 Lloyd George pushed through the Government of Ireland Act, which purported to establish "parliaments" in Dublin and Belfast. These parliaments were in reality to enjoy little more than the powers of local self-government but it was still a momentous step forward. The partition of Ireland between the Protestant North and the Roman Catholic South was an implicit part of the scheme, but Lloyd George privately hoped that, when the time came, the patent absurdity – both political and economic – of establishing two Irelands, would lead to a last-minute change of heart on the part of Ulster and that some sort of compromise would be reached which would preserve the

Union yet appease Protestant fears of being overwhelmed in a Catholic Ireland.

Any number of ingenious formulae might be put forward in London but in the long run it was the Irish, whether from the North or the South, who had to be satisfied that an acceptable solution was on offer. In May 1921 James Craig, scion of a wealthy whiskey-distilling family and leader of the Ulster Unionists, met de Valera in a Dublin suburb. Both literally and politically he was taking his life in his hands, but the venture paid off: there was no meeting of minds, still less any full agreement, but both men came to the conclusion that a settlement of some kind might be possible. A fresh impulse, however, was needed to get negotiations under way. It came, rather unexpectedly, from King George V. "The King is an old coward," Lloyd George had written contemptuously when the Lord Mayor of Cork was engaged in an ultimately fatal hunger strike. "He is frightened to death and is anxious to make it clear that he has nothing to do with it." Frightened or not, within a few weeks of Craig's meeting with de Valera, the King opened the new Northern Ireland Parliament in Belfast with a passionate appeal to all Irishmen "to pause, to stretch out the hand of forbearance and conciliation, to forgive and forget, and to join in making for the land they love a new era of peace, contentment and goodwill". The general lines of his speech had, of course, been agreed in advance with his ministers in London; the fervour and palpable sincerity with which he spoke was his own contribution. Forgetfulness, in fact, was more than could be hoped for but it was in an atmosphere of forbearance and conciliation that de Valera agreed, after some prevarication, to impose a truce on his army of freedom-fighters and to open formal negotiations with the British government.

Over the previous years Michael Collins had established himself as a bold, resourceful military commander of the I.R.A. Though he hesitated formally to acknowledge the fact, however, he knew that de Valera was unequivocally the Irish leader in the struggle for independence. Lloyd George at first underestimated de Valera. He was not a big man, he told his secretary, Tom Jones, but he was "a sincere man, a white man and an agreeable personality". The Prime Minister got it badly wrong. De Valera was by far the biggest man on the Irish scene, big physically as well as spiritually for he stood six foot one and was built like the rugger player he had been in his youth. He was sincere in the sense that he held strong views and made no secret of them, but he did not hesitate to equivocate or make promises that he knew he could never keep if he thought it expedient to do so. His personality was generally agreeable but he could be exceptionally unpleasant if thwarted or offended. What exactly Lloyd George meant by "white man" is uncertain, but the phrase suggests a straightforwardness and lack of subtlety which was far removed from de Valera's nature. It was not long before Lloyd George realised that he was up against a formidable adversary, whose resourcefulness and ingenuity matched his own.

It quickly became apparent that their views, if not incompatible, were far apart. In a nutshell, Lloyd George offered independence within the Commonwealth, de Valera wanted independence *tout court*. It was the same thing, Lloyd George insisted; Ireland would have exactly the same measure of freedom as Canada and Australia. Surely that was enough to satisfy anyone? Canada and Australia were huge and thousands of miles away, de Valera retorted; Ireland was small and on England's doorstep. What was real independence for a distant dominion would be virtual subjugation for Ireland. Lloyd George explained that, whatever his own feelings on the subject, an offer of complete independence outside the Commonwealth would not be acceptable to his Cabinet, let alone the House of Lords. That was Lloyd George's problem, retorted de Valera; he had equally determined followers who would not allow him to accept any halfway house. In this he was being disingenuous; he was uneasily conscious of the fact that a large proportion, probably more than half of his supporters, would be content with what Lloyd George seemed to be offering. What was worse, he suspected that Lloyd George was nearly as well informed about the state of public opinion in Ireland as he was himself. The British knew that, for every extremist member of Sinn Féin who would oppose any compromise which infringed the principle of complete independence, there was another who would accept it with equanimity. Half a loaf, these moderates believed, would be better than none; the three-quarters of a loaf that was on offer were still more acceptable. Even among de Valera's less tractable followers there was the comforting awareness that whatever settlement emerged from London need only be a halfway house. If Ireland proclaimed its complete independence in 1921, war with England would possibly, perhaps even probably follow. If, on the other hand, Ireland accepted the dominion status that was on offer and then, a few years later, began to disengage itself from any surviving imperial ties, it would be difficult if not impossible for the English to take any effective steps to impede its progress. Such arguments did not entirely satisfy de Valera, but the fact that they were accepted by many patriotic Irishmen convinced him that it would be politically dangerous to refuse even to consider compromise. With some public professions of scepticism and much private agonising, de Valera agreed that talks in London should begin.

The mood in London was little more enthusiastic. The formula that de Valera had used when accepting the invitation to a conference had been markedly non-committal: the Irish would come "with a view to ascertaining how the association of Ireland with the community of nations known as the British Empire may be reconciled with Irish national ambitions". Could this be compatible with the dominion status that London was prepared to grant? Was the phrase "common citizenship" to which London attached so much importance something that could be reconciled with "Irish national aspirations"? If not, could some other acceptable formula be devised? And if the negotiations foundered on some such issue as whether citizenship should be "common" or "reciprocal", would the British public be ready to support a war inspired by what they might feel to be a trivial semantic issue? It was no doubt a great thing that the Irish were coming to London, but how disastrous it might be if they went away embittered and empty-handed.

* * *

Who would the Irish send to conduct the negotiations? Lloyd George took it for granted that de Valera himself would lead the team; so, for that matter, did almost everyone in Dublin. The only man who thought otherwise was de Valera himself. It would be better for him to remain in Dublin, he said, where he would be well placed to sell to the Irish people the sort of compromise that was likely to emerge. Besides, if he was not himself immediately involved in the talks it would give the other members of the team a breathing-space in which they could plead that they were referring questions back to their principals in Dublin. These points had some validity but his principal motive was less altruistic. However successful the delegates might be it seemed likely that there would be aspects of the settlement which would offend, even outrage, large parts of the Irish population; which would, indeed, offend and outrage de Valera himself. The Irish Prime-minister did not wish to be too closely associated with such compromises; indeed, he considered it possible that he would wish to disown the settlement altogether. If the delegates came back with a settlement that gave Ireland the reality but not all the trappings of independence, de Valera would be able to take advantage of their efforts by assuming effective power himself, while simultaneously denouncing them for betraying the true interests of their country. His position was hardly noble but from the point of view of his own personal future, even perhaps Ireland's future, it made good sense.

The Irish delegation, de Valera decreed, must be led by his only serious rival, the man who had made his name as the most stalwart of those who had gone into battle against the British, Michael Collins. According to Batt O'Connor, one of Collins's intimates, his friend and leader was horrified by the proposal. It was an unheard-of thing, Collins protested, that "a soldier who had fought in the field should be elected to carry out negotiations". He saw, as clearly as de Valera, how damaging the role of negotiator could be to anyone who went to London and returned with anything less than complete independence; he also genuinely believed that he was ill-suited to the sort of late-night haggling over the choice of words which would inevitably be an important part of the London meetings. He was out-manoeuvred, however; reluctantly he acknowledged de Valera's authority and accepted that it was his duty to undertake the task.

After Collins, the most important member of the delegation was Arthur Griffith, the founder of Sinn Féin and the man who was to succeed de Valera as President in 1922. Griffith and Collins, de Valera believed, though traditionally militants, were also realists who would be likely to strike a deal even at the cost of sacrificing sacred principles. As a counter-weight he included Robert Barton, one of his most loyal followers who had been part of the original group that had opened negotiations in London. The other members of the team were relative light-weights; important as any was the Secretary of the delegation, Erskine Childers, an Englishman by birth who had become an intemperate champion of total Irish independence and was eventually to perish at the hands of a Free State firing squad.

From the beginning the status of the delegation was ambiguous, a circumstance which was to be the cause of dissension and much bloodshed in the future. The Dáil, the Irish parliament in Dublin, ruled that its emissaries should be given a free hand and should not be required to report back for approval before agreeing terms. De Valera, in principle, supported this, but he later issued a letter of instruction which provided that the plenipotentiaries should report back to the Cabinet in Dublin before a final deal was done. His own preferred solution, given that the unqualified independence to which he aspired would not be available, in the short term at any rate, was "external association", an ill-defined arrangement by which Ireland would enjoy complete internal independence and would formally cease to be a member of the Commonwealth, but would retain certain Commonwealth links, be represented at its conferences and accept some obligations when it came to the harmonisation of foreign policies.

The serious negotiations began on Tuesday 11, October, 1921. The arrival of the Irish delegation in Downing Street was a dramatic affair, its path lined by a host of well-wishers "reciting the rosary, singing hymns, exclaiming good wishes, pouring blessings on the difficult undertaking". There was no doubt that almost all those who turned out for the occasion *wanted* a settlement to be reached; more significantly, it seemed that a substantial majority *expected* a settlement to be reached. No-one doubted that there would be hard bargaining, but the fact that things had got as far as they had, that a British prime minister was actually sitting down with the Irish leaders, was taken to be an assurance that both sides were ready to make concessions and that a compromise acceptable to everyone would eventually be reached. The negotiators themselves were less confident. *The Times* reported that there was a "complete lack of optimism" when the meetings began. "It is no secret," declared that newspaper, that Lloyd George "after his encounters with Mr de Valera, was afraid that he would be dealing with idealists and theorists whom it would be impossible to bring down to the discussion of hard and concrete political facts." Perhaps if de Valera himself had headed the Irish delegation it might have been more difficult to make progress: "It is like sitting on a merry-go-round and trying to catch up the swing in front," Lloyd George had complained, after a particularly protracted session with the Irish leader. Collins, however, was a different matter – more business-like, more realistic, and more ready to search for verbal formulae that would satisfy the susceptibilities of both sides without sacrificing any fundamental principles.

Over the next three or four weeks there followed a welter of plenary sessions, conferences, sub-conferences and private meetings between individuals on either side. Collins was un-equivocally the Irishman to whom the British delegates paid most attention, with Griffith the only man who approached him in stature. Both men were formally committed to full independence and nothing less; both men were in fact resigned to the need to accept some sort of second-best. But would an acceptable second-best be on offer? Lloyd George had given them cause for hope, but would he be able to carry the day against his more intransi-gent colleagues? The most important of these was the Lord Chancellor, Lord Birkenhead. As F. E. Smith, Birkenhead had been known as one of the most turbulent champions of Ulster's rights and an ardent opponent of any move towards Irish independence. Was it possible that he would now prove more conciliatory? Austen Chamberlain, leader of the Conservative Party in the House of Commons, was another significant player. He seemed disposed to concede the government in Dublin a high degree of self-rule but he was known to oppose with passion any suggestion that Ireland should renounce the monarchy and quit the Commonwealth. No less intractable in this respect was the Colonial Secretary, Winston Churchill. Churchill, while at the War Office, had been conspicuous in his insistence that any civil disorder in Ireland should be suppressed swiftly and by force. Was it possible that he would now be prepared to contemplate any serious derogation of British rule? Given the personalities involved, the Irish had good reason to be sceptical; but when it came to the point they discovered that Birkenhead, Chamberlain and Churchill had tacitly abandoned their more intransigent positions. Provided the principle of some sort of British overlordship could be maintained, they were resigned to making considerable concessions on the practicalities. The Irish were not pushing at an open door, but they were pushing at a door which was far less securely fastened than they had originally believed.

* * *

The Irish delegates did their best to keep in touch with their Cabinet in Dublin and to ensure that any concessions they might be forced to make would be deemed acceptable both sides of the Irish Channel. When it came to the point, however, it proved difficult either to persuade Dublin of the realities of the situation or to extract any clear or precise instructions. "Dublin is the real problem," Collins wrote angrily. "They know what we are doing, but I don't know exactly the state of their activities." It began to seem more and more likely that de Valera and his wing of the party expected the delegates to make the necessary concessions to secure independence but wanted to be free to disown any such behaviour and to claim that they had never understood how far Collins and his fellow negotiators had planned to go. Collins continued to plead with de Valera that he should belatedly join the negotiators in London; de Valera continued to protest that it was his duty to remain in Dublin. It was painfully obvious to Collins that he was being set up as a scapegoat, but in the last resort, he concluded, this was a risk with which he had to live. His job, as he saw it, was to get the best terms that he could for Ireland. If he destroyed his reputation in the process then that was a price that must be paid; the independence of his country was more important.

The position of the British delegation was little more comfortable. Lloyd George knew that a substantial element of the Conservative Party disapproved heartily of the fact that he was treating with the rebels; that he should allow these same rebels to renounce their allegiance to the Crown was unthinkable. In the last resort the negotiations turned on one simple and fundamental issue: the Irish found it almost impossible to accept a situation in which their country, however independent in practice, remained formally part of the British Commonwealth and subject to the British monarchy; the British would not accept anything else. A degree of compromise was possible but in the end someone had to give way. It was the Irish who did so. In the eyes of posterity their sacrifice might seem very small – they were accepting no more than a largely illusory and, as it turned out, temporary limitation on their independence. At the time it seemed a matter of critical importance. "I may have signed my political death warrant," said Chamberlain as the final deal was done. "I may have signed my actual death warrant," retorted Collins ruefully. Eight months later he was ambushed and murdered on the road to Cork.

Until the very end there was doubt whether the gulf between

the two parties would finally be bridged. "Once again the Irish Conference seems to have reached deadlock. The fate of the negotiations trembles in the balance," reported *The Times* gloomily on the morning of December 6. "The government have gone to the extreme limit of generous concession. Upon the point of allegiance there can be no compromise, no concession and no argument." But even as this dire pronouncement was casting gloom over the breakfasts of many millions of British readers, the final steps to resolve the crisis were being taken in Downing Street. The previous day, Lloyd George, perhaps in a mood of reckless impatience, more probably with cool calculation and possibly some connivance with his opposite numbers, had issued an ultimatum. Things could drag on no longer: if the Irish could not now accept what was on offer, it would be war. As a final inducement, Lloyd George threw in an extra concession over Ireland's right to manage its own taxes. It was enough. Whether or not the Irish took Lloyd George's threats altogether seriously, they reckoned that there was no more to be gained by further intransigence. Even then there was a trace of uncertainty until the very last moment. The Irish left Downing Street for a final confabulation, were expected back by 10.00 p.m., and caused consternation by delaying their return by a further hour. It was twenty past two in the morning before the document was finally signed: Lloyd George; Austen Chamberlain; Birkenhead; Churchill; the Secretary for War, Worthington Evans; the Chief Secretary for Ireland, Hamar Greenwood, and the Attorney General, Gordon Hewart, for the British; Collins, Griffith, Robert Barton, E. J. Duggan and George Gavan Duffy for the Irish. When the two teams had originally met they had taken their seats on different sides of the table with barely a nod to the other parties. Now they shook hands. It was over.

* * *

It was not over, of course. In some ways it had hardly even begun. To most people the announcement that agreement had been reached was a cause for delight. "I am overjoyed to hear the splendid news," the King told Lloyd George. "I am indeed happy in some small way to have contributed by my speech in Belfast to this great achievement." An achievement it certainly was, and one that deserved celebration, but the final signature had hardly been put before its limitations became distressingly evident. The Irish delegates, de Valera and the other hardline republicans maintained, had exceeded their brief; they should have referred back to their Cabinet before concluding the deal; in no way were they justified in sacrificing the principle of a republic and settling for this servile halfway house. When the matter was put to a vote the republicans lost by a narrow margin, but de Valera was having none of it. He resigned as President, stood for re-election, was defeated and balefully withdrew; declaring that he was prepared to "wade through blood" to achieve the republic.

Whose blood? There was much disorder in the North – more than fifty civilians, rather more Catholics than Protestants, were murdered in March 1922 alone – but it was in the South that full-blooded civil war broke out, between those republican rebels who maintained that the Treaty with Britain was unacceptable and must be overturned, by force if necessary, and the official government which accepted the settlement and was determined that law and order should be maintained. In the long run it is hard to say who was the victor, in the short term the rebels lost and the Free Staters, supported with British arms, won. Yet de Valera survived, his position precarious but his standing, in the hearts of his followers at least, substantially unimpaired. In 1932 he became Prime Minister of Ireland, and in 1937 Ireland became a republic, but it would only be in 1949 that Ireland finally severed its links with the Commonwealth, the ostensible reason for the republicans having rejected the Treaty almost thirty years before.

So was the agreement signed in the early hours of 6 December, 1921, which had seemed of such momentous importance at the time, in fact of ephemeral significance, no more than a fleeting phase in the sad history of Anglo-Irish relations? Certainly it did not provide the conclusive solution to which the negotiators had aspired. But after it, nothing was the same. Until the end of 1921 whatever happened in Ireland had been a British responsibility: British blood might not have been shed; British money, even, might not have been expended; but in the last resort the buck had stopped in Whitehall. Once the Treaty had been signed, all this was changed. The existence of Ulster as part of the United Kingdom made it inevitable that there would be friction between Dublin and London, the geographical presence of Ireland between Britain and the Atlantic ensured that it could not be ignored when questions of national defence were being considered, but what happened in Eire was no longer a responsibility of the British. For some this was a cause for regret, for many more an immense relief. The seven hundred and fifty years of rule from London had not been happy ones – for the Irish subjects or for their British overlords.

NOTES FOR FURTHER READING

J. J. Lee's *History of Ireland between 1912 and 1935* (Cambridge 1989) provides as excellent account of the period before and after the signing of the Anglo-Irish agreement. Tim Pat Coogan has written biographies of de Valera (London 1933) and Michael Collins (London 1990). Lord Longford's *Ulster* views the story from another angle.

3

ULYSSES

1922

On 2 February, 1922, after innumerable vicissitudes, James Joyce's Ulysses *was finally published in book form. With it, said T. S. Eliot, Joyce had "killed the nineteenth century". Since Eliot's own poetic masterpiece,* The Waste Land, *appeared later the same year, 1922 was indeed an annus mirabilis in modernist English writing.*

* * *

The word "English" is used only in a literary sense. Joyce would have been disconcerted and probably displeased if accused of being an Englishman. He was born in 1882, sharing a birthday with the future Irish Prime Minister and President, Eamon de Valera. Joyce found the coincidence entirely acceptable: if pressed he would have pronounced himself a patriotic Irishman. The greater part of his writing was set in Dublin and most of his characters, though occasionally with exotic overtones as in the Jewish blood of Leopold Bloom, were identifiably Irish men and women. Loyalty towards his native land, however, did not extend so far as to make him feel that he ought to spend any length of time there. He left Ireland in 1902, returned briefly in 1904, and otherwise lived entirely on the mainland of Europe.

James Joyce holding what must have been one of the first copies of *Ulysses* (painting by Jeffrey Morgan).

Though in his writings he did full justice to the miseries that traditionally afflict the clever and sensitive schoolboy, he seems in fact to have been something of a success: popular, good at games, happy to conform with the overpowering religiosity which pervaded the mainly Jesuit teachers. At home he was equally contented: under the leadership of his talented but feckless father his family stumbled from financial crisis to financial crisis, but nobody starved and the background was not so unstable as to prevent him excelling academically. With little noticeable effort – indeed, with a conspicuous effort to avoid the appearance of making any conspicuous effort – he coasted his way through school and University College, Dublin, and emerged with little formal academic distinction but the reputation of being the cleverest student of his year.

The reputation was deserved, but meanwhile his popularity had faded. He had a handful of close friends but most of his contemporaries, and his teachers as well, seem to have found him insufferable. His brother Stanislaus, a less brilliant but much nicer man, thought he was like Steerforth in *David Copperfield*. Joyce was more aware of the feelings of other people and curious about their personalities and predilections than Steerforth's enormous self-satisfaction permitted, but he was still capable of great arrogance. His mind, he once told Stanislaus, "was of a type superior to and more civilised than any he had met up to the present". The fact that his self-satisfaction was, on the whole, well justified makes it no less unattractive. W. B. Yeats, who with some reservations, admired both Joyce and his works, referred to the young man's "colossal self-conceit": like many of those who knew Joyce in the late nineteenth century he felt certain that he would go far but was not certain in what direction and in any case felt no strong urge to accompany him along the way.

If he had chosen to do so, Yeats could have been pretty certain that he would be called upon to subsidise his indigent friend at frequent intervals. Like many men of genius, Joyce faced constant financial problems and took it for granted that it was the duty of lesser mortals to extricate him from his difficulties. "I am going alone and friendless into another country," he told Lady Gregory as he prepared to visit Paris to study medicine, "and I am writing to know can you help me in any way?" She could and did, but Joyce's most constant victim was Stanislaus whom he pillaged relentlessly, taking it for granted that his brother's pay packet would be available for his needs and treating his possessions as his own.

The difference, of course, between James Joyce and a hundred other consistent spongers is that Joyce was dedicated and hard-working and that it was quickly evident that his writing was of brilliant and sustained originality. The greatest obstacle in his road to popular success lay in his reluctance, inability almost, to compromise. He knew what he wanted to say, he knew how he wanted to say it; if others had different ideas, then so much the worse for them. Such an attitude was admirable and, he being Joyce, entirely defensible, but it did not make life easier for a young and struggling author. "I can't print what I can't understand," protested the editor of a literary magazine when confronted by what would eventually become *A Portrait of the Artist as a Young Man*. In the end many publishers were to accept Joyce's work even though they could not fully understand it, but the indulgence that was eventually to be extended to an acclaimed master was not so readily available when he was still a young unknown.

In fact there was little that was obscure about Joyce's first published prose work, *Dubliners*: a series of exquisitely crafted *nouvelles* – short stories without a story – depicting episodes in Dublin's daily life and the ordinary yet triumphantly individual characters who walked its streets. Nor, by contemporary standards at least, was there anything obscene about the book, but this did not stop timid publishers from expressing their fears that there would be trouble if they handled such incendiary material. Joyce was outraged. "Your suggestion that those concerned with the publishing of *Dubliners* may be prosecuted for indecency is, in my opinion, an extraordinary contribution to the discussion," he told one offender. "I know that some amazing imbecilities have been perpetrated in England but I really cannot see how any civilised tribunal could listen for two minutes to such an accusation against my book." This did not stop a series of publishers – including Mills & Boon – deciding that *Dubliners* was too hot to handle. With an ill-judged appreciation of the monarch's reading habits, Joyce appealed to King George V for his support; unsurprisingly the King's private secretary replied that it was "inconsistent with rule for His Majesty to express his opinion in such cases".

Possibly the excisions that Joyce reluctantly made were enough to satisfy the censor, possibly the material had never been as combustible as the publishers feared, at all events the publication of *Dubliners* caused barely a frisson of disapproval. Joyce was relieved but at the same time slightly disappointed: disappointed because he enjoyed a row but also because sales were poor and the critics did not pay his work as much attention as he felt it deserved. Such reviews as appeared were for the most part unenthusiastic. More significantly, however, Joyce gained some important new admirers. For Joyce the most valued – if only because he greatly admired Pound's work – was the pioneer of Imagism and high priest of the *avant-garde*, Ezra Pound. Pound was immensely influential and his review of *Dubliners* in the monthly literary magazine *The Egoist*, hailing Joyce as an innovator of real importance, did more than anything else to convince serious critics that here was a new voice that they should not ignore.

It was to Pound that Joyce showed the early chapters of his next book: a largely autobiographical account of the artistic development of a young Irishman, Stephen Dedalus, in Dublin at the end of the nineteenth and beginning of the twentieth centuries. The response was immediate and enthusiastic. *A Portrait of the Artist as a Young Man*, felt Pound, was "damned fine stuff . . . clear and direct like Mérimée." The right way for it to be published, initially at least, was, he believed, chapter by chapter in *The Egoist*. Joyce was happy to agree. He was living in Trieste at the time, scratching a rather precarious living by giving English lessons to the children of the city's richer and more intellectually ambitious families: he was more than ready to accept whatever Pound thought best. The first three chapters of *A Portrait* were duly published, the editor professed herself satisfied with the response from her readers, all seemed to be running smoothly. Then, on 28 June, 1914, the Archduke Franz Ferdinand of Austria was assassinated in Sarajevo. Within a few weeks a minor tragedy escalated into war. Joyce found himself marooned in a country in which he was an alien and possibly – for the authorities were not very clear about the status of Irish citizens – an enemy alien to boot. His position was precarious and, to add to his problems, the post between Trieste and London became erratic and he could not be sure that *The Egoist* would receive his material in time for the next monthly issue. It was September 15 before the final instalment had been published. By then the problems of wartime shortages were beginning to become evident. Though a few admirers felt that Joyce had made a significant advance and had reinforced his claim to be taken seriously, it proved difficult to find a publisher ready to produce the material in book form.

Their caution could be forgiven. The sales of *Dubliners* had been, if not derisory, then certainly far less than Joyce had hoped; he had been due to receive royalties on any copies sold after the first five hundred; by the end of 1915 there had been only thirty or so such sales. In wartime paper was hard to obtain, publicity more hard to come by, even the most idealistic publisher might reasonably hesitate to take on a book which offered such limited prospects of financial success. Grant Richards, who had finally published *Dubliners* and had been promised first refusal of *A Portrait*, did not feel inclined to throw good money after bad. Secker, Herbert Jackson, Duckworth all politely refused. Finally, the editor of *The Egoist* gallantly volunteered to produce as a bound book the chapters which she had already printed in her magazine. It was not as satisfactory as being taken on by an established publisher but it was a great deal better than nothing. Once again it was Pound who supported Joyce when his morale was low. "I think the book is permanent like Flaubert and Stendhal," he told the author. "I think you join on to Hardy and Henry James – I don't mean a resemblance, I mean that there has been nothing of permanent value in prose in between." Joyce badly needed such reassurance. His novel, he could not forget, had not merely been rejected by every publisher to whom it had been offered, but twenty printers in England and Scotland had then refused to print it for fear of prosecution. The financial returns from his writing had so far been pitifully small. "I receive nothing in the way of royalties," he told the Royal Literary Fund when W. B. Yeats, Ezra Pound and other literary notables put his name forward for a grant. Their efforts secured him £75: much more considerable a sum than it sounds today but still unlikely to sustain him for any serious length of time.

By now Joyce had moved to Zurich. The war hardly impinged on his consciousness except in so far as it made travel and communications more difficult. One of the reasons why the Royal Literary Fund was hesitant about awarding him a grant was that they suspected him of being insufficiently patriotic. In this they were fully justified. If only because so many Irishmen were fighting for King and country against the Germans, Joyce hoped for an Allied victory, but he did not feel personally involved. He had never had anything to do with public affairs, "extreme or otherwise", Yeats assured the Literary Fund, "and I think disliked politics. He always seemed to me to have only literary and philosophical sympathies. To such men the Irish atmosphere brings isolation, not anti-English feeling." He was not, would never be, did not wish to be part of the British literary establishment. Almost without noticing it, however, he was acquiring some status as a recognised and respected figure. In 1916, for the first time, he was awarded an entry in *Who's Who*: a sure indication that, even if he had not yet fully arrived, he was well on the way. *A Portrait* was greeted by reviews that, while sometimes hostile, treated the book as a work of real significance. H. G. Wells complained about its obscurity but acknowledged that it was "a book to buy and read and lock up but . . . not a book to miss". Joyce rejoiced in the attention, good or bad: very reasonably considering that it was better to be insulted than ignored. And all the time he was gestating the work that was to win him a place among the immortals.

* * *

Joyce had conceived the idea of *Ulysses* more than ten years before the book finally appeared. Initially it was to have been a short story; gradually it grew. When his Aunt Josephine complained that there was much in it that she could not understand, Joyce retorted: "I *told* you to read the *Odyssey* first." It would probably not have helped her much if she had. *Ulysses* was indeed inspired by and in a loose way modelled on Homer's *Odyssey* but any readers hoping that their schoolboy recollections of the Greek epic would guide them through a dense and sometimes intractable narrative would be likely to find themselves disappointed. "It is my system of working," replied Joyce obscurely when asked why he had called his novel *Ulysses*. He told one of his pupils that he had been fascinated by the *Odyssey* since he had first read it at the age of twelve. He found the subject of Ulysses "the most human in world literature". Its spirit permeates his book. But though Stephen Dedalus, a survivor from *A Portrait*, is patently

Telemachus, and Leopold Bloom, the Jewish advertising man, stood for Ulysses, Joyce allowed his characters personalities of their own without worrying too much how closely they corresponded to their Homeric counterparts. The book is about Dublin as much as it is about any individual. "For myself I always write about Dublin," said Joyce, "because if I can get to the heart of Dublin I can get to the heart of all the cities of the world." The style is luxuriant and complex, sometimes wilfully obscure: "I've put in so many enigmas and puzzles that it'll keep the professors busy for centuries arguing over what I meant," wrote Joyce with some satisfaction. Nowhere was this more true than in Molly Bloom's great closing monologue, the first sentence of which contained 2,500 words. The prose is not impenetrable but to penetrate it requires resolution and close attention. The fact that the effort is worthwhile shows that Joyce was not merely a good writer but a great one.

The problems that Joyce had already encountered, with the authorities eager to censor anything that seemed even tenuously salacious, were redoubled when it came to *Ulysses*. "This is the most beautiful thing we'll ever have!" exclaimed the editor of the *Little Review* when offered the earlier chapters for publication in her magazine. "We'll print it if it's the last effort of our lives." It almost was. A succession of printers had to be approached before one could be found who would take on something that was likely to provoke damaging criticism if not prosecution. When it came to publication in book form the prospects seemed still less promising. Even Leonard and Virginia Woolf, noted for the liberality of their opinions, hesitated to accept something that, they felt, "reeked with indecency". At first it was thought that publication in the United States would be easier but this optimism was shaken when the U.S. Post Office confiscated and burnt four copies of the *Little Review* because of the extracts from *Ulysses* that the magazine contained. In February 1921 the case came to court and the editors of the *Little Review* were found guilty and fined. The amount of the fine itself was trivial but the costs involved in fighting the case were far greater and the judgment was enough to deter the *Little Review* from publishing any further extracts. The prospects of bringing out *Ulysses* in book form in either Britain or the United States seemed more remote by the day. Then Sylvia Beach, a friend and admirer of Joyce who owned and ran Shakespeare and Company, a small and adventurous English language bookshop in Paris, volunteered to print a thousand copies and distribute them around the world. Ezra Pound, André Gide, W. B. Yeats, Ernest Hemingway: all subscribed. Bernard Shaw refused to do so but in terms that could only encourage sales. "It is a revolting record of a disgusting phase of civilisation," he told Sylvia Beach, "but it is a truthful one . . . It is some consolation to find that at last somebody has felt deeply enough about it to face the horror of writing it all down and using his literary genius to force people to face it."

The element in *Ulysses* which attracted the most attention and, in some cases, was most roundly condemned was Joyce's use of the "stream of consciousness" technique, the interior monologue, in which the reader encounters the thoughts and feelings of a given character without the apparent intervention of the author or any kind of external analysis. Joyce did not invent the interior monologue nor was he the only author to exploit it – Marcel Proust and Virginia Woolf among his approximate contemporaries were both adept in its use – but he pushed it to the limit – sometimes, some would say, beyond the limit – of comprehensible communication. "Modernism" is a term that covers many bold experiments and revolts against the established literary order – Eliot, Pound, Yeats, Woolf can all claim to be among its more energetic exponents – but with *Ulysses* and later, still more, with *Finnegans Wake*, Joyce established himself as one of the most ambitious, perhaps the most ambitious, of its practitioners.

It was far from universally acclaimed. Many would-be readers complained that *Ulysses* was largely incomprehensible and that the bits that could be comprehended were either dull or obscene, sometimes both. Joyce's father thumbed through a few pages, then remarked "He's a nice sort of blackguard!" and put the book away. The judgment, if he had heard of it, would have cost the author few sleepless nights, nor would he have been unduly concerned by the denunciation of the *Sporting Times*, which declared that, in writing *Ulysses*, Joyce had "ruled out all the elementary decencies of life and dwells appreciatively on things that sniggering louts of schoolboys guffaw about . . . The main contents of the book are enough to make a Hottentot sick." Joyce's surprise was that the *Sporting Times* had seen fit to mention the book at all, not that they had done so in such offensive terms. If he had known of it he might have been more disturbed by the judgment of Virginia Woolf, recorded in her diary, that she found it "an illiterate, underbred book . . . egotistic, insistent, raw, striking and ultimately nauseating". Even abuse from such a quarter, however, would not have dented his confidence: to have bruised the sensibilities of Mrs Woolf was something with which Joyce could live, the important thing was that she should have read *Ulysses*, taken it seriously and discussed it with her friends. That *Ulysses* should be universally loved and admired was too much to hope for – perhaps even was positively undesirable – that it should be read and talked about was what mattered.

Read, talked about and bought; but to be bought it had to be available in the bookshops. The problems that the *Little Review* had encountered when it published *Ulysses* episode by episode were redoubled when the complete book was circulated. In London the Director of Public Prosecutions acquired a copy and found it rich in "glaring obscenity and filth". Customs were instructed to intercept and destroy any copies that were imported from France, if they slipped through the net and were exhibited in the bookshops then the police were encouraged to intervene before the British public was hopelessly corrupted. In the United States the authorities were no less alive to this threat to public morality: in December 1922 five hundred copies of the second edition of *Ulysses* were seized and destroyed. Though its fame spread until *not* having read *Ulysses* became a reason for shame in intellectual circles, it was not until 1934 that the United States Court of Appeal finally ruled that, even though certain passages were of extreme vulgarity, they were nevertheless "sincere, truthful, relevant to the subject and executed with real art". We think, the judges concluded, that this is "a book of originality and sincerity of treatment and that it has not the effect of promoting lust" and that, therefore, although it might offend many readers, it did not "fall within the statutory definition of obscenity".

* * *

After all these vicissitudes, the formal first publication of *Ulysses* in February 1922 probably did not seem to Joyce so much a defining moment as it does for the literary world today. Apart from anything else, as is so often the case when a book reaches the reviewers and the bookshops, the author's interest had already moved on to his next project. In fact Joyce did not write the first sentences of what was cautiously entitled *Work in Progress* until the spring of 1928 but the book that would finally emerge as *Finnegans Wake* had been gestating in his mind long before that. Any hopes on the part of his more traditional admirers that *Ulysses* represented the high point of Joyce's modernist ambitions must have been dented when Joyce first proposed as a working title for a collection of articles on his current work: *"Our Exagmination round his Factification for Incamination of Work in Progress"*. He knew that he was retreating, or perhaps advancing, into a world of ever more intense obscurity and in some ways he regretted it, since he knew that he was losing touch with a body of literate and intelligent readers who were eager to admire and enjoy his work. H. G. Wells for one had hitherto been among his more ardent champions, but he saw *Work in Progress* as being "a dead end. . . I can't follow your banner any more than you can follow mine." "But the world is wide," Wells continued comfortingly, "and there is room for both of us to be wrong." The problem was that almost everyone thought Joyce was the wronger of the two. When the seven hundred pages of *Finnegans Wake* were finally published in 1939 the *Sunday Times* announced that it proposed to ignore the entire enterprise as being "irrelevant to literature". Most of the newspapers that got round to reviewing it did so in dismissive terms; in the *Observer* Oliver

Gogarty concluded that it was "the most colossal leg-pull since Macpherson's *Ossian*". There were those who hailed it as a triumph but they were few: if *Finnegans Wake* is a masterpiece it remains one of the least read and least understood masterpieces in literary history.

No-one would claim that, for its part, *Ulysses* was widely read or easily understood. By any standards it demands patience and unwavering concentration. But in the current of twentieth century literature it stands like a great rock which cannot easily be passed by. To ask whether Joyce was a greater writer than Faulkner, Hemingway or E. M. Forster is a fatuous question, as pointless as asking whether Jane Austen was a greater writer than Charlotte Brontë or Flaubert than Stendhal. What is certain is that he cannot be ignored. *Ulysses* was a landmark. It influenced the course of serious fiction writing as no other novel of the twentieth century. It can be criticised, challenged, disliked, but like its author it cannot be ignored.

NOTES FOR FURTHER READING

The classic biography of James Joyce is that by Richard Ellman (London 1959). A vast literature has accumulated about Joyce; perhaps the most interesting for the general reader is that by Anthony Burgess: *Joysprick: An Introduction to the Language of James Joyce* (London 1965).

4

THE BURNING OF SMYRNA

1922

13 September, 1922. The ancient city of Smyrna, once the greatest port of the Eastern Mediterranean, was ablaze. Hundreds of thousands of would-be refugees crowded the harbour, desperately seeking to escape the flames. In the harbour warships from Britain, France, Italy and the United States floated impotently while their crews watched the horrific scenes on land. It was a night that nobody present, whether victim or spectator, would remember without a sense of horror.

* * *

Nowhere did the calculations of the peacemakers of Paris come more quickly unstuck than in the Middle East. They had assumed that the Ottoman Empire, long past its prime, was now totally defunct. Their task, as they saw it, was to carve up the corpse in a way that would satisfy the victors; the fact that the corpse itself might have different views was not something they even considered. Even at the time there were those who doubted whether the negotiators had either the wisdom or the knowledge to reach a conclusion that might prove permanent. "After 'the war to end war'," remarked the future Field Marshal Wavell, "they seem to

H.M.S. *Iron Duke*, flagship of the Mediterranean Fleet,
watches impotently while Smyrna burns.

have been pretty successful in Paris at making a 'peace to end peace'."

But the fundamental assumption on which the Allies based their calculations seemed reasonable enough. The Ottoman Empire really was in a sorry state. It had been born several hundred years before, the creation of waves of nomadic horsemen who had emerged from the depths of central Asia, Muslim by faith, Turkish – in a variety of forms – by language, itinerant by nature. They were not true empire-builders, in the sense that they had neither the inclination nor the ability to create stable, prosperous and perhaps, in the long run, self-governing communities, but they were conquerors who exploited the lands which they had overrun and repressed ruthlessly any attempts on the part of their victims to regain their independence. Their territorial ambitions were limitless, and their achievements fell little short of their ambitions. At its zenith the Muslim Empire made the astonishing achievements of Byzantium seem almost modest: it occupied vast tracts of Europe, extending to the walls of Vienna and to the Crimea; it spread through Egypt and along the North African coast; it embraced almost all that we now think of as the Middle East.

But these glories were long past. By the end of the nineteenth century most of its European territories had been lost; its grip on North Africa was becoming ever more tenuous; Egypt was to all intents and purposes run by the British. Even in Constantinople, at the heart of the Ottoman Empire, racial minorities demanded special privileges and the rule of the centre seemed each year more shaky.

Then, in 1914, came the Great War. Turkey had no reason to

become involved: it would have made better sense for it to have remained aloof, extracting whatever profit it could from the misfortunes of the losing side. Instead, it went to war and, still more ill-advisedly, backed the wrong horse. By the end of 1918 its army had been routed, its economy was in ruins. The Sultan, never the most effective of rulers, had been robbed of most of his authority. Small wonder that the victorious Allied powers took it for granted that they should dismember what was left of the Ottoman heritage. At the Peace Conference various solutions were propounded. The most drastic would have swept the Turks from Europe and placed Constantinople and the Straits under some sort of international control. This was the approach favoured by the British Foreign Secretary, Lord Curzon. His Prime Minister, Lloyd George, was not prepared to go so far but accepted that the Greeks, who had, albeit rather belatedly, fought on the Allied side, should be rewarded for their efforts by being granted much of the Aegean coast of Asia Minor and its hinterland. This was not unreasonable – racially the area contained a heady cocktail of nationalities but the Greeks probably comprised the largest element. The Americans could therefore congratulate themselves on having reached a solution in accord with President Wilson's celebrated principles. The Treaty of Sèvres, drawn up in May 1920 and formally signed three months later, left Constantinople to the Turks but put the Straits under international control. The Turkish army was limited to some 50,000 men and its financial affairs were subjected to the supervision of an Inter-Allied Commission. The Aegean coast, including the great city of Smyrna, was put under Greek control for five years, after which the inhabitants would be allowed to decide their own future. Few can have doubted that the Greeks would use their period of overlordship so as to ensure that, when the time came, the inhabitants would vote to remain with Greece. The terms of the Treaty of Sèvres were, of course, deeply distasteful to the Turks, but this, if anything, made them more attractive in Allied eyes; certainly Turkish susceptibilities did not figure largely in the minds of the negotiators. Yet even as early as this there were some who doubted whether a permanent solution had been found. The French President, Raymond Poincaré, wryly remarked that it was only right that the Treaty should have been signed at Sèvres, famed for its manufacture of delicate porcelain: "It too is a fragile object. Perhaps a shattered vase." He was not the only Allied statesman to doubt whether the settlement could survive for long. Winston Churchill expressed that uncertainty in typically flamboyant phrases: "Loaded with follies, stained with crimes, rotted with misgovernment, shattered by battle, worn down by long disastrous wars, his Empire falling to bits around him, the Turk was still alive."

* * *

Perhaps more correctly, *a* Turk was still alive. There are not many Napoleonic figures of whom it can be said that, single-handedly, they changed the course of history, but if there had been no Mustapha Kemal, known to posterity as Kemal Atatürk, it is hard to believe that Turkey could have recovered so quickly and so dramatically from its defeat. Atatürk was a professional soldier of conspicuous ability who had established himself as a national hero in the Gallipoli campaign in 1916–18 and in time was to transform Turkey from an incompetent and antiquated satrapy to a modern state. In April 1920 he had just been elected leader of the newly formed national assembly in Ankara. At first all did not go smoothly; indeed, after the first few months, it seemed that Atatürk had come and gone before he had had a chance truly to establish himself. In savage fighting in the hinterland of Smyrna the Turks were routed by a better-trained and better-equipped Greek army. "The Turks," proclaimed Lloyd George in the House of Commons, "are broken beyond repair." So they might have been if the Greeks had been allowed to exploit their advantage, but the Allies took alarm at developments which they felt might altogether destroy the balance of power in the Middle East, and brought the Greek offensive to a halt. Atatürk survived to fight another day.

That day was not long delayed. Towards the end of August 1922 there was another short but fierce war between Greece and Turkey. This time it was the Greeks who were routed. Five divisions were almost totally destroyed, fifty thousand prisoners taken. What was left of the Greek army fled pell-mell towards the coast, hoping to find ships that would enable them to escape. As they retreated they burnt and pillaged the villages through which they passed. They paid little attention to whether their victims were Greek, Turk or Armenian; it was enough that they were witnesses to the fleeing army's humiliation and potentially might offer shelter to the Turkish pursuers. The victorious Turks, relatively well-ordered and restrained compared to their defeated enemies, advanced through scenes of hideous desolation. By the time that they arrived at the gates of Smyrna they were in a vengeful mood.

* * *

The city that they were approaching was among the most ancient and civilised, as well as the most important, in the Middle East. It boasted one of the finest natural harbours in the Mediterranean; its hinterland was a rich producer of tobacco, grapes, figs and other fruits; it provided a beginning and an end for the most important trade routes between East and West. Though the largest element of its population was Greek it was markedly cosmopolitan and the various racial elements co-existed in harmony. Its clubs, hotels, bars, gardens and stately homes made it a place where it was pleasant as well as profitable to live. In the past it had endured troublous times, most notably in the fifteenth century when it had been razed to the ground by Tamburlaine, but for several hundred years it had prospered in notable tranquillity. Now, suddenly, it found itself exposed to an imminent threat with which, neither militarily nor psychologically, was it equipped to cope.

Smyrna had, in fact, already been given a taste of what was to come. In May 1916, incensed by the fact that German coastal guns had been shelling British ships in the bay of Smyrna, the Royal Naval Air Service dispatched two bombers to attack the residential areas of the city. A few days later there was a second strike. By the standards of the Second World War, by the standards even of the German attacks on London between 1915 and 1918, the damage done was negligible: twenty or thirty houses destroyed, perhaps a hundred people killed or injured. To the inhabitants of Smyrna, however, it seemed a terrifying presage of what might be to come. Yet in the end nothing more *did* come, there were no further attacks, the city relapsed into its habitual calm. When the Greeks occupied Smyrna some three years later they found that they were taking over a city that seemed almost entirely unscathed by war.

If they had known the fate that awaited their city it is possible that even the Turkish citizens of Smyrna would have settled for a tranquil if ignoble existence under Greek rule. The Greeks initially seemed anxious to make this as palatable as possible to their Turkish subjects. "The enthusiasm filling our hearts is fully justified," warned a senior officer, "but any improper manifestation of this enthusiasm would be entirely out of place." But Greek control of Smyrna depended on their continued military domination of the Turks, and by September 1922 it was obvious that this no longer pertained.

As the defeated Greek armies fell back on Smyrna they devastated the towns and villages through which they retreated, partly to deny any facilities to the Turkish invaders, partly out of spite. It does not seem that the destruction of Smyrna itself was part of the same deliberate strategy. Most reports suggest that the fires were started either by accident or by Turkish soldiers. This does not seem to have been been the result of any policy decision: it is unlikely that the Turkish authorities should have sought systematically to destroy a city which they had just conquered and whose facilities they hoped to enjoy. Discipline was lax, however, and there were many Turkish soldiers who were happy to avenge the casualties their army had suffered by looting and setting fire to deserted properties. Whatever shadowy Greek authority survived had neither the facilities nor the inclination to check the blaze: most of those who should have taken the lead in extinguishing the fires had chosen instead to flee the city.

After a long drought and with a strong wind blowing, what could have been a few minor fires quickly merged into a mighty conflagration. The population, which had derived a false sense of security from the presence in the harbour of warships from the world's leading powers, now saw those ships as being their only possible salvation. They flocked to the harbour in search of sanctuary. Probably only a few hundred people died in the fire itself, but thousands, perhaps tens of thousands, died on the waterfront or drowned in a vain attempt to reach the allied ships. The toll in terms of human suffering could hardly have been more fearful.

NOTES FOR FURTHER READING

There is a plethora of material on this subject. Marjorie Dobkin's *Smyrna. 1922* (London 1988), Giles Milton's *Paradise Lost* (London 2008) and David Fromkin's *A Peace To End All Peace* (London 1989) are three books on which I drew heavily. Patrick Kinross's admirable biography of Atatürk (London 1964) is highly relevant, as is Harold Nicolson's *Curzon. The Last Phase* (London 1934) and Winston Churchill's *The World Crisis. The Aftermath* (London 1929).

5

THE DEATH OF LENIN

1924

On the evening of 21 January, 1924, at ten minutes to seven, Vladimir Ilyich Lenin stirred slightly in his bed, groaned once and died. He had been gravely ill for nearly a year, barely conscious for several hours. In political terms his death made little difference to the governance of his country: for the average Russian it was the most momentous event since the ending of the First World War. It was the passing of a god.

* * *

God had come a long way in his fifty-four years on earth. Lenin's father had been an inspector of schools, a respectable but undramatic occupation which gave Lenin neither the affluent start that might have helped him in his career nor the right to boast about his plebeian and impecunious origins. As a child he was volatile and mischievous, quick to learn but slow to make friends and with a touch of malice that tainted all his relationships. His father died, suddenly and unexpectedly, when Lenin was only sixteen and, though the family was hardly on the breadline, he found himself bearing responsibilities for which he was ill prepared. He showed no early interest in politics and, when his

Lenin and Stalin together on a bench – probably *circa* 1920.

brother Alexander became involved in a half-baked plot to assassinate the Tsar and ended up on the gallows, he seems to have concluded that Alexander had chosen the wrong path and that he would under no circumstances make the same mistake. The authorities, however, decided otherwise: as Alexander's brother he found himself deemed guilty by association, arrested and interrogated on the most spurious grounds, and dismissed from his university for no good reason. Almost against his will his mind was opened to new ideas and he soon fell under the spell of that most potent of revolutionary works, Karl Marx's *Das Kapital*. By the late 1890s he had become a committed and proselytising Marxist. He soon fell foul of the law, and exile in Siberia was followed by years of wandering around Europe, including a lengthy stay in London. It was at that time, in October 1902, that he met one of the two men with whom his life was to be most inextricably enmeshed, the brilliant, erratic and irrepressible Leon Trotsky. Trotsky was then the coming man, whose fiery revolutionary tracts had earned him considerable renown. As such he was a well-known figure throughout Russia, but his power was insubstantial and the apparently unshakeable Tsarist regime seemed to have little reason to take him or any other dissenter very seriously. It took catastrophic defeats in the war against Germany to weaken the Tsarist grip and open the way for revolution. Even then, it seemed that Lenin would be sidelined, marooned in Zurich while new men took power in Petrograd. It appeared that he had missed his chance: and then the Germans, in April 1917, conceived the idea of using him as a secret weapon against his country and dispatched him, in Winston Churchill's words, "in a sealed truck, like a plague bacillus, from Switzerland into Russia". He arrived by way of Finland, fearful that he would be arrested when the train steamed into Belo-Ostrov; instead he was greeted as a hero and hailed as the most plausible successor to the Provisional government which ruled precariously in Russia.

One man who did not meet him at Belo-Ostrov, though he was at pains subsequently to rewrite history so as to make it appear that he was prominent among the welcomers, was Joseph Stalin. Stalin was some ten years younger than Lenin. He came from more or less the same stratum of society, but, unlike Lenin's family, his was scarred by bitter hatreds and his parents treated him at the best neglectfully, at the worst with conspicuous cruelty. Physically too he was warped, almost deformed. Such disadvantages, when combined with high intelligence and a passionate determination to succeed, were likely to produce a man who would be at least a disruptive force in society, perhaps even a monster. He was both. *Tout comprendre*, they say, *est tout pardonner*, but while one can understand the forces that made Stalin what he was, it is impossible to pardon the atrocious tyranny which later brought so many millions to death or misery.

Stalin first met Lenin at a Party conference in Finland in 1905. He claims that his immediate reaction was one of disappointment: Stalin had expected to find a prodigy, instead he saw a "man of the most ordinary appearance, below average height and in no way distinguishable from ordinary mortals". It did not take him long to realise that he was in fact meeting one of the most extraordinary of mortals. The time would come when Stalin would view Lenin as an irritating relic of the past, an unnecessary obstacle to his own advancement, but he never wholly shed a certain reverence for the older man. Without Lenin, he accepted, the course of the revolution would have been far less certain; perhaps, indeed, it might never have taken place at all.

The two men had much in common in their vision of the future of Russia, indeed of the world, yet in their personalities they were very different. Both believed passionately that the struggle would not be over until Communism had become the accepted form of government throughout the world but for Stalin such a world must necessarily be dominated by Soviet Russia. Lenin, of course, took it for granted that Russia would be a major, probably *the* major power in a Communist world but he contemplated with resignation if not with equanimity the existence of Communist countries that would not inevitably look to Moscow for their daily orders. Even within the territories of the former Russian empire Lenin was prepared to accept the establishment of independent republics; a concept which to Stalin seemed unacceptably divisive. Both men were thirsty for power, the more absolute the better, but Lenin saw power first and foremost as a means of achieving a truly socialistic Russia. Stalin aspired to the same conclusion, but for him power was something which he craved for personal ends as well. Stalin wanted to be a dictator, in part at least to gratify his own ambition; Lenin wanted power because of what he could do with it to change the world. Though both men were autocratic and ready to impose the Communist way of life upon the peasantry, by force if necessary, Lenin was prepared to leave time for persuasion and accepted that the peasants had some rights that should not lightly be overridden. Stalin almost rejoiced when he encountered opposition because of the occasion which it gave him to repress it with brutal force. Lenin genuinely believed in the dictatorship of the proletariat and expected that, under Communism, the state would gradually wither away until individual freedom was achieved. Stalin paid lip-service to such ideals, but it was painfully evident that no state over which *he* presided would ever experience any significant withering of its powers. Stalin's object was to destroy totally so that he could rebuild; Lenin preferred to reconstruct and only to destroy when his ends could be achieved in no other way.

It was Lenin who played the leading part in the putsch which led to the ejection of Kerensky's interim government and the installation of a Communist regime. It was Lenin who became chairman of the new Council of People's Commissars – "Sovnarkom" – which from October 1917 was to govern Russia. Trotsky was the next most prominent in the list of the Commissars, Stalin at that time was still relatively inconsiderable, appearing last in the list of the Councillors as the people's commissar of nationalities. Whoever might be in charge, the West at first paid little attention to the convulsions that were reshaping Russia. The only thing that mattered was whether the new government could be persuaded to continue to play a part in the war with Germany; the exact form of the ill-conceived and no doubt temporary administration which was ruling in Moscow seemed relatively unimportant. It soon became evident, however, that Russia did *not* intend to continue hostilities and that the new regime was likely to endure, for some years at least. The statesmen of London and Paris surveyed the so-called Communist government and decided that they did not like what they saw. "Civilisation is being completely extinguished over gigantic areas," protested Churchill, "while Bolsheviks hop and caper like troops of ferocious baboons amid the ruins of cities and the corpses of their victims!" He demanded that the West should intervene to suppress the baboons before they fully established themselves. Lloyd George thought that this would be singularly ill-advised. Bolshevism, he agreed, was to be deplored but any attempt to emancipate Russia by foreign armies would be likely to prove disastrous, as much for the would-be liberators as for the Russians: "To send our soldiers to shoot down the Bolsheviks would be to create Bolsheviks here." This sensible counsel was ignored and the worst possible compromise adopted: the West intervened in sufficient force to unite the Russians in opposition to the invaders but not on a scale that would provide any effective relief to the White Russian forces, who at one time had seemed capable of mounting a successful counter-revolution.

* * *

It would be extravagant to claim that Lenin mellowed with old age, but traces of humanity did begin to appear in what had previously been a machine of terrifying and barbarous efficiency. Towards the end of the civil war he began to view his fearsome acolyte with some distaste. He saw in Stalin the quintessence of the calculating ruthlessness which had marked his own rise to power and he no longer felt sure that in post-war Communist Russia these were the proper attributes of leadership. Though firm documentary evidence is hard to come by, it seems likely that in the last years of his life Lenin was striving to ensure that it was Trotsky, not Stalin, who would succeed him.

He had left it too late. Stalin combined to devastating effect the skills required to build up a powerful political machine, along with a bluff and straightforward jollity that convinced the world – or at least his less perceptive admirers – that here was a man who was demonstrably straightforward, who put the interests of the nation ahead of any personal ambitions. "Comrade Kartotekov" – "Comrade Card-index" – was his nickname among his colleagues; a tribute to the obsessive thoroughness with which he checked and counter-checked the strengths, weaknesses and likely loyalties of those with whom he worked. The honest "Uncle Joe" who was to win the confidence of Franklin Roosevelt a quarter of a century later was already exercising his charms in the early years of revolutionary Russia. Lenin was not taken in, still less was Trotsky, but to the rank and file of the Soviet Communist Party it seemed that here was a man in whom they could have total confidence. In January 1923 Lenin belatedly began to move for the ejection of Stalin from his post as Party General Secretary. If he had been in the full possession of his powers he might still have had his way but he was already a sick man. Stalin knew that if he could only hold on for a few months until Lenin had finally vanished from the scene, he would be safe. "I love him with all my heart!" he wrote to Lenin's sister; a protestation which, if ever it got to Lenin's ears, would have been greeted with some scepticism. It was not entirely hypocritical – Stalin was never wholly to throw off the reverence which he had felt for his former mentor – but that love did not stop him working assiduously in the last few months of Lenin's life to ensure that Lenin's real opinions, in particular his views on the qualities of his most likely successor, did not become widely known.

He succeeded; in the last months of Lenin's life Stalin ensured that the man who was still theoretically his leader was kept almost entirely isolated from the outside world. The curious thing is that Trotsky, who must have known that Lenin favoured him for the succession and would, if given a chance, have proclaimed as much overtly, did nothing to strengthen his claim. It almost seemed that he had lost his nerve, had decided that supreme power was something to be feared rather than sought after. By hanging back, he ensured his own eventual destruction. Stalin was not a man who would accept the existence of a potential rival, however much that rival might protest that he was ready to serve as a loyal subordinate. In due course Trotsky was expelled from the Party, exiled and eventually murdered.

Lenin's final years, as he saw effective power ebbing away and became ever less able to assert his will, must have been tragically unsatisfying. Alex de Jonge, in his admirable biography of Stalin, has compared Lenin to King Lear in whom "understanding and weakening grew together". Lenin's perception of what was necessary if Russia was to develop into the sort of country which any right-minded citizen might aspire to live in, grew only when it was too late for him to bring it about. He recognised that there could be no such evolution if Stalin remained General Secretary, inevitably inheriting absolute power or something very near to it. "I propose," Lenin wrote in something that was close to his last will and testament, "that a way be found to remove Stalin . . . and to replace him with someone else who differs from Stalin in all respects, someone more patient, more loyal, more polite, more considerate to comrades, less head-strong." The trouble with this otherwise admirable proposition was that no-one who was patient, considerate and polite stood any chance of checking the ferocious driving-force that lay behind Stalin's rise to power. By the time he died Lenin must have realised that the governance of Russia was likely to fall into the hands of a man whose vision of the future was far removed from anything that he had grown to believe was most desirable.

Likely but not certain. To the less perceptive Kremlin-watchers it still seemed that Trotsky was the most natural inheritor of Lenin's mantle. He was the best known, the most popular: only his own political ineptitude and the superior tactical skills of his rival made it possible for Stalin first to isolate and finally to destroy him. Even then, Zinoviev and Kamenev among the other Communist leaders were at least as prominent as Stalin. It was only the latter's mastery of the machinery of government, the skill with which, working invisibly from within, he built up unchallengeable support among the Party membership and grew to dominate first the Central Committee, then the Politburo, that made the succession his.

Lenin died before the process was complete, but Stalin contrived to turn even that event to his own advantage. On the day of Lenin's death Trotsky was out of Moscow, travelling by train to the Black Sea. Stalin cabled him the news, regretting that it had been felt necessary to hold the funeral almost immediately, leaving no time for Trotsky to return. In fact he gave the wrong date: Trotsky would have had ample time to get back to Moscow and play a prominent part in the ceremonies involved in Lenin's interment. To the outside world it seemed as if he could not be bothered to attend. Stalin was left to hold the centre of the stage and to protest his grief with passionate eloquence. The last major obstacle in his rise to supreme power had been removed. "Stalin was jubilant," remembered his private secretary. "I never saw him in a happier mood than in the days following Lenin's death."

Lenin had already been revered, now he was worshipped. His body was not buried or cremated but reverently embalmed and placed in a vast mausoleum where the people could pay tribute at his shrine. Petrograd, once St Petersburg, now re-emerged as Leningrad. Stalin, of course, was prominent among the mourners. The first honour guard who stood beside Lenin's coffin consisted of Zinoviev, Kalinin, Kamenev and, inevitably, Stalin (Trotsky, of course, was conspicuously absent). When the coffin was carried out of the House of Trade Unions to Red Square it was carried by six carefully selected peasants and, once again, Zinoviev and Stalin. On the following day, as all over Russia sirens wailed, locomotive whistles sounded, guns boomed their salute, the coffin was carried to the shallow vault which had been hastily prepared for it. Stalin was prominent among the bearers. It must have given him some wry amusement thus to foster the cult of the man who had provided the only significant obstacle to his rise to power. In life Lenin had threatened to be Stalin's nemesis; in death he became his tool.

Even then Stalin's accession to power was by no means a foregone conclusion. "Lenin's Testament", containing as it did strictures on his would-be successors' abilities and powers of leadership, put the triumvirate of Kamenev, Stalin and Zinoviev in a difficult and potentially embarrassing position. They reacted by restricting its distribution and suppressing public discussion. There was still room for Trotsky to make a come-back or for one of the other leading figures to assert his primacy. Possibly they thought it would be too dangerous, possibly they were genuinely anxious not to rock the boat at a moment when Russia had been destabilised by the loss of its patron saint: at all events they remained quiescent while Stalin built up the tally of his supporters in the Central Committee and the Secretariat. By the time that, at the Fourteenth Congress at the end of 1925, they rallied their forces to oppose the take-over of the Party and the country, it was too late; Stalin had so far established his position that the battle was lost before it was properly begun. One by one his possible rivals were destroyed. Zinoviev was the victim of a particularly ferocious assault. He was accused of wilfully misinterpreting the needs and aspirations of the peasantry. "This is wobbling, not politics," Stalin asserted. "This is hysterics, not politics." His speech was greeted by applause so enthusiastic that his opponents realised that his position was impregnable. All they could do was acquiesce sullenly and await their eviction from office and, more often than not, as in the cases of Zinoviev and Kamenev, their eventual execution or, as was the fate of Trotsky, murder.

* * *

If Lenin had not fallen so desperately ill at a crucial moment, if he had lived a few more years, if he had succeeded in forcing Stalin into the side-lines and promoting another, more temperate successor, would the history of Russia, of the world, have been very different? Probably not: Russia would still have been a Communist society, operating through oppression and determined to impose collectivisation on a reluctant peasantry. There would still have been much misery and discontent. It is hard to believe, though, that any other ruler could have been so dictatorial, so callous, so supremely indifferent to the sufferings of his victims. In the end the Soviet Union would have been the victim of German aggression, it could not have escaped the horrors of the Second World War: if it had been spared Stalin, however, then the 1920s and 1930s might have been very different and the lot of the Russian peasantry more tolerable than the reign of Joseph Stalin made possible.

NOTES FOR FURTHER READING

The works of Robert Service, particularly *Lenin: A Biography* (London 2000) and *A History of Twentieth-Century Russia* (London 1997) are of pre-eminent importance. I have also made much use of Robert Payne's *The Life and Death of Lenin* (London 1964) and Alex de Jonge's excellently written *Stalin and the Shaping of the Soviet Union* (London 1986).

6

SPAIN INVADES MOROCCO

1925

On 8 September, 1925 a Spanish army under the supreme command of the effective dictator of Spain, Miguel Primo de Rivera, and spearheaded by a contingent from the Tercio de Extranjeros, the Spanish Foreign Legion, went ashore in Alhucemas Bay, on the Mediterranean coast of Morocco. Leading the Tercio was a young and recently promoted colonel, Francisco Franco.

* * *

Primo de Rivera was indeed a dictator, but unlike many of his kind he was a dictator who listened to other people and occasionally allowed them to influence his actions. Usually this proved a strength; sometimes the voices to which he listened would have been better left unheard. In the case of Morocco, he had begun by feeling that any involvement in North Africa would prove a waste of time, money and, probably, human lives; in time he became, if not an ardent imperialist, then at least an advocate of military intervention to protect national interests and to expunge a Spanish disgrace.

In spite of the tiny distance which divided Spain and North Africa, there had been few significant incursions into Morocco

Spanish soldier guarding the coastline following the landing at
Alhucemas Bay.

before the end of the nineteenth century. Primo de Rivera was not the only man to find the country unappealing. A fertile but narrow coastal strip rapidly gave way to the barren and thinly populated mountains of the Rif. Few in number though they might have been, however, the Arabs who lived there were far more ready and able to defend their territory than the predominantly black inhabitants of the rest of Africa. With so little to gain and so high a price to pay it was unsurprising that, in the rush for territory, the European imperialists of the nineteenth century tended to look further south for richer and easier pickings. This could not last, however, and once Britain, Spain, France and Germany – to mention only the European countries most actively involved in North Africa – began to pay serious attention to the area, it became evident that the obstacles in the way of a would-be conqueror were less daunting than had at first appeared. In theory the country was united under the rule of a Sultan in Fez; in practice his sway extended over less than a quarter of the country and the rest belonged to largely independent and usually warring tribes. Not much effort would be needed for European imperialists to establish their rule over the greater part of the country, either expelling the present Sultan or, if he proved amenable, employing him as a puppet who would take his orders from the colonial powers.

Britain and France both fancied that they had claims to establish themselves as effective rulers of Morocco but it suited them better to install Spain as the effective ruler of the north of the country. The Germans were the losers; they blustered and sulked and in July 1911 sent a gunboat to protect their commercial interests, but in the end they accepted that it made better sense for them to concentrate their colonial pretensions on the vast area which they had acquired in the Congo far to the south. The First World War extinguished their presence in Africa and by the early 1920s Spain was left, in its own eyes at least, as the effective ruler of the greater part of Morocco. "In its own eyes" is an important qualification. Whatever deal the Spanish, French and British might hatch together did not involve consultation with the Arab inhabitants of the country and it was rapidly becoming evident that Arab resistance was likely to be both courageous and tenacious.

Courageous and tenacious, but not united. Dislike of the Spanish might have been common to most of the Arabs in Morocco but dislike of their fellow Arabs was little if at all less prevalent. The Spanish could take comfort from the fact that no Sultan, let alone any other tribal leader, seemed likely to inspire the sort of nationalist fervour that might seriously threaten their position. Then, in 1920, a former teacher and civil servant called Abd el-Krim, who had earlier fallen foul of the Spanish authorities and been imprisoned for anti-colonial activities, took alarm at the incursions of Spanish troops into what were still effectively independent tribal areas and set out to unite the tribes of the Rif in opposition to the invaders. General Silvestre, who had been nearly ten years in command of the Spanish forces in Morocco and had learnt to treat Arab resistance with – till then not wholly unjustified – contempt, dismissed this new threat as being of trivial importance. Abd el-Krim, he said, was a nonentity, unfit to command a platoon, let alone to lead an army against the Spaniards. He saw no reason to revise this opinion when a Spanish detachment some 250 strong was ambushed and largely destroyed by the Rifians at Abarran: the local commander had been guilty of gross negligence, he concluded, and had brought his destruction on himself; he, Silvestre, would lose no time in restoring the proper order of things. He grossly underestimated both the size and the fighting ability of Abd el-Krim's army and was forced to order a retreat. The retreat soon became a rout, his army was virtually wiped out, Silvestre himself died with almost all his staff. The defeat at Anual cost the Spaniards nearly twenty thousand dead and effective control over most of Eastern Morocco. More important than that, in the eyes of Primo de Rivera at least, it cost the Spanish army its reputation. Perhaps more important still, it struck a fatal blow at the already shaky reputation of the Spanish government. The *coup d'état* which brought Primo de Rivera to power in Spain in September 1923 could never have taken place if the debacle in Morocco had not prepared the way.

* * *

Primo de Rivera might have doubted the wisdom of colonial adventures in North Africa but now it was the honour of the Spanish army that was at stake. Anual must be avenged, and avenged at once: he promised the Spanish people a "quick, dignified and sensible" end to the troubles in Morocco. The more chauvinistic among his supporters were dismayed when the first step towards such an end proved to be the withdrawal of what was left of the Spanish presence in the interior of Morocco to positions nearer the coast. "*Réculer pour mieux sauter*" is an established principle of warfare but it is not likely to seem attractive to a population smarting under the indignity of military defeat at the hands of what they saw as a savage rabble. Nor did it win the immediate approval of the young and ambitious commander of the *Tercio*, Francisco Franco.

Franco had been brought up in a miserably unhappy family, with a father who was a brutal libertine and a mother who reacted by adopting an exaggeratedly austere religiosity. He was the runt of the litter, ignored or, worse still, bullied by his macho brothers. When he joined the army his diminutive size – he stood only five feet, three inches – and his shrill and squeaky voice seemed to mark him as a potential victim for bullying. Nor did his record as a military cadet (he passed out 250th from an intake of 312) suggest that he was on the path to greatness. Gradually, however, his fearlessness, his capacity for hard work and his total dedication to the military order led to his rising from the ruck of young officers and his acceptance as a coming, perhaps even *the* coming man. He believed that the Spanish presence in Morocco must not only be maintained but restored in its entirety and was dismayed when Primo de Rivera proposed to abandon a large part of those territories still in Spanish hands. It is a tribute to his determination (and also to Primo's readiness to listen) that the policy was to some extent revised and the withdrawal reduced in its scope.

It is possible, even probable, that the Spanish would never have been able to undertake the recovery of their former possessions if Abd el-Krim had not become involved in a war with the other great colonial power in Morocco – France. The French saw Abd el-Krim's growing stature as a threat to their own position: they concluded that he should be destroyed before too many of the tribal chiefs had rallied to his banner and while there was still an effective Spanish presence in the area. He played most obligingly into their hands: it was Abd el-Krim who was the first to attack, and though he may have believed that, in so doing, he was merely pre-empting a French offensive, he nevertheless managed to present himself as an aggressor rather than the victim of an imperialist assault. Abd el-Krim hoped that the tribes of French Morocco would hasten to join a war of liberation; he was disappointed, most of them hung back to await the outcome, some even concluded that the French devil they knew was better than the Rif devil they did not and actively supported the colonial power.

By the middle of 1925 the Franco-Spanish forces in Morocco could claim that the Rifian attack had been checked if not yet decisively defeated. An essential element in the counter-attack was to be a Spanish landing on the Moroccan coast in Alhucemas Bay, a hundred miles or so to the east of Gibraltar. Once safely ashore, the expeditionary force would be well placed to strike at Abd el-Krim's capital at nearby Ajdir or to drive his armies back into the mountainous interior. It did not seem likely that the invasion would be confronted by much in the way of coastal defences but as soon as the news of the landings reached the Moroccans it was inevitable that they would rush all the troops that were available to the danger area. "Spain cannot keep on maintaining her soldiers on cliffs which it is costly to supply," Primo de Rivera had observed a year before. It was essential, therefore, that the initial landings should be in such force that the invaders would be able not only to maintain themselves in the case of what could be a formidable counter-attack but push on rapidly into the interior.

A fleet was assembled at Cauta and Melilla, ports respectively well to the west and east of the area controlled by the rebels. In their diversity and ramshackle appearance the ships that carried the invaders looked more like the motley argosy that rescued the allied armies from Dunkirk in 1940 than the highly professional armada that returned them to Europe some four years later. The almost wilful amateurism extended to the operation itself; the ships entered the bay with lights blazing and the troops on board singing lustily. Indeed, the Spaniards were almost disastrously casual: the landing craft which carried Franco and his Legionaires grounded in the shallow waters and the final assault had to be made by troops wading ashore, sometimes up to their necks in water, holding their weapons above their heads in a sometimes unavailing effort to keep them dry. At one point their plight seemed so desperate that a general retreat was ordered. Franco, who calculated that as many if not more lives would be lost if they fell back than if they pushed on, and who anyway believed that to call off the operation would have a calamitous effect on the army's morale, ignored the order. He was proved right. Losses were not light, well over a hundred Spanish troops lost their lives, but within two hours of disembarkation more than eight thousand men were ashore and consolidating their position. If things had gone wrong Franco's career would have been at an end; as it was he was the hero of the day. The fighting was ferocious and neither side was disposed to behave with charity towards its adversaries. The Moors already had a reputation for taking few prisoners and treating those that they did take with some brutality; the Spaniards were resolved to give as good – or as bad – as they got. "Those who resisted too much were put to the knife," was the grim comment in Franco's diary. *"Viva la muerte!"* – "Long live death!" – was the battle-cry of the *Tercio*; on that September day they showed why no other call to arms would have suited them so well.

Even though the Spaniards had established themselves on the mainland the battle was by no means over. It was two days before the vigorous counter-attacks were beaten off, a fortnight before Primo de Rivera ordered a general advance. But by then, though the war was not over, the war was won. With 25,000 French troops in the field and the Spaniards pushing forward from Alhucemas Bay, Abd el-Krim was doomed. He fought gallantly but in the end was forced to sue for peace. The Sultan, in truth no more than a puppet ruling at the behest of the invaders, was confirmed as ruler of all Morocco. Abd el-Krim surrendered to the French – not unreasonably assuming that if he fell into the hands of the Spanish he would be unlikely to escape with his life – and was eventually sent into exile on an island in the Indian Ocean. Even after his departure from the scene Moroccan resistance spluttered on but it was no more than a guerrilla operation, a nuisance to the triumphant West but in no way a serious threat. By 1927 the protectorate had been pacified. It was 1956 before it eventually graduated to full independence.

Primo de Rivera was the hero of the hour but his hour proved short. When he seized power in 1923 he had genuinely believed that this would be no more than a brief interlude after which Spain would re-emerge as a full and true democracy. Somehow, that moment never seemed to come. As happens so often with dictatorships, the government, with the plea that it was essential if law and order were to be maintained, arrogated ever-increasing powers to itself. It was dependent on the tolerance, if not the active support, of the army, yet alienated the officers by imposing reforms that were sensible in themselves yet seemed revolutionary to those who were affected. The economy turned sour and fierce inflation weakened what was left of middle-class support. In spite of this, Primo was not so much driven from office as sickened of the battle and voluntarily left the field. He took himself into exile, settled in Paris and died within a few months.

His former henchman, Francisco Franco, did not allow himself to become involved in Primo's travails. Instead, he devoted himself to nurturing his anyway highly successful military career. By 1935 he had become Chief of Staff of the Spanish army. More than any other individual he was responsible for the coup of July 1936, in which the army offiers launched the civil war that ravaged Spain for the next two years. Long before that war ended, the army commanders, desperate to achieve unified direction, had entrusted Franco with supreme powers. They deluded themselves that this was a temporary expedient. Perhaps at first Franco thought the same, but as with his former mentor, Primo de Rivera, the time never seemed expedient to call it a day. He remained as absolute ruler of Spain until his death in 1975.

NOTES FOR FURTHER READING

David Woolman's *Rebels in the Rif* (London 1968) provides an excellent picture of Morocco during this turbulent decade. So far as the principal protagonists are concerned, the best source on Abd el-Krim is his memoirs, published in two volumes: *Mémoires d'Abd el-Krim* and *Mémoires II: la crise franco-marocaine* (Paris 1927 and 1984). *Fascism from Above: the Dictatorship of Primo de Rivera* (Oxford 1983) by Shlomo Ben-Ami and Paul Preston's *Franco. A Biography* (London 1994) are good studies of their respective subjects. Raymond Carr's *Spain 1808–1975* (Oxford 1982) provides the best overall picture of the period.

7

THE GENERAL STRIKE

1926

"A General Strike is not an industrial dispute. It is a revolutionary move which can only succeed by destroying the government and subverting the rights and liberties of the people." This somewhat partisan presentation of the facts by the editor of the Daily Mail proved to be the catalyst that provoked the very phenomenon which he had deplored. The printers refused to set the offending passage. Stanley Baldwin considered their behaviour amounted to wilful interference with the freedom of the press – the freedom in question, of course, being that of the proprietors to decide the policy of their papers rather than that of the journalists and printers to maintain their own point of view. The Labour Party, though as reluctant as the Conservatives to associate themselves with anything that might seem to smack, however remotely, of revolution, found themselves willy-nilly forced to support the rebellious printers.

Outside an inconsiderable extremist fringe on either side, there was no enthusiasm for a confrontation. Some of the employers, indeed, felt some sympathy for the other side: "Try living on their wages before judging them," was George V's lapidary comment. The Unions, though more united in the justice of their cause, were no more eager to go to war. Economically and politically it seemed that a General Strike would be bound to shake the fabric of society and

Police and demonstrators jostle during the General Strike.
The photograph does not suggest that there was any deep
animosity on either side.

bring the nation to the brink of civil war. To the average Briton it must have seemed inconceivable that this would ever be allowed to happen. And then, at a minute to midnight on 3 May, 1926, the inconceivable occurred: the Trades Union Congress called a General Strike.

* * *

And the world seemed to go on, if not "just the same", then at least with no notably cataclysmic consequences. There was, in fact, no reason for the "average Briton" to be quite so much taken aback by the crisis. There had been a dress rehearsal for a General Strike less than ten years before. Again it had been the miners who were to the fore. A collapse in the price of coal, coupled with a retreat by the government from any direct involvement in the running of the industry, led to an attempt on the part of the pit owners to make the miners work longer hours for less pay. The miners refused to oblige, the owners closed the pits and settled down to starve the miners into submission, the miners called on their traditional allies, the dockers and the railwaymen, to join them in a strike that would, in effect, bring Britain to a standstill. On that occasion it had been the miners' nerve that had cracked; the General Strike was called off before it had had any serious effect, the miners held out for a few weeks and then in effect surrendered, accepting terms which were certainly no better and in some ways were even worse that those that they had been offered at the beginning.

Move on eight or so years. The economic and social balance of the country had not significantly altered. A quarter of the population still owned nearly three-quarters of the nation's wealth, less than 1 per cent of children at elementary schools went on to university. There had been important changes, though. One of the most notable was the growing strength and unity of the Trades Union Congress. A disciplined and determined response to the demands of the employer, a distant pipe dream in 1921, now seemed a real possibility. And once again it was the miners who had led the charge. It is impossible not to sympathise with their cause. They were doing a job that was always unpleasant and sometimes dangerous, for a wage that offered them little more than bare subsistence. Yet, in fairness to the employers, it must be admitted that they were not growing fat on the fruits of the miners' tribulations. Once, indeed, coal had been the source of vast wealth for the owner, but this was largely in the past. Most of the coal produced in Britain each year cost more to mine than it was worth on the market. The viability of the mining industry depended on the subsidies that, in one form or another, it received from the government, and Stanley Baldwin's Conservative regime was showing increasing reluctance to involve itself in any way in the running of the industry. If they were to survive, the owners must put their house in order, and the most obvious ways to achieve that were either by reducing the size of the labour force or by paying each miner less – better still both at once.

Baldwin was anxious to keep the government as far as possible detached from the bickering and haggling that would be inevitable if any deal was to be struck between miners and pit-owners. More than most members of his Cabinet, in particular the pugnacious and rambunctious Winston Churchill, he saw that there were two sides to the dispute and was as ready to urge compromise on the employers as on the employed. But, though well-disposed, he was an easy-going man who shrank from confrontation. Certainly no decisive intervention could be expected from him. If there was one man who, as an individual, could radically have changed the process of negotiation it was the architect of the Transport and General Workers Union – the T.G.W.U. – the redoubtable Ernest Bevin, and Bevin, though no firebrand, had no doubt that battle must be joined and that, even though at great cost to the union members, the battle could be won.

Even without Bevin, however, by the early spring of 1926 the move towards a general strike had gained a momentum that made it more or less unstoppable. The T.U.C. was prepared to envisage the possibility of a reduction in wages, but only as part of a package that would involve the owners also accepting a loss of income – in theory temporary but potentially extending far into the future. The unions were convinced that they had been conciliatory almost to a fault. "We have striven, we have pleaded, we have begged for peace. We still want peace. The nation wants peace," expostulated J. H. Thomas, probably the most influential and certainly among the more conciliatory of union leaders. The employers would have retorted that they wanted peace quite as much as the T.U.C. but that, though they had gone to the limit of what was economically possible, some would have said even beyond it, their offers had been contemptuously rejected.

Many, both on the Left and on the Right, believed that a general strike could easily prove to be a precursor of civil war. Baldwin was less alarmist. "Everything that I care for is being smashed to bits at this moment," he protested, "but that does not take from me either my faith or my courage. Before long the angel of peace, with healing in his wings, will be among us again."

It was to be some time before the angel of peace was given a chance to work his wonders. The proclamation of a state of emergency put the country onto what was, to all intents and purposes, a wartime basis. In the centre of London this was particularly noticeable. Hyde Park was closed to the public and transformed into a camp for the troops who were drafted in to cope with any possible violence and a base where supplies of food could be accumulated and then distributed around the capital. The railway stations virtually closed down, building sites were deserted, scarcely a single bus left its depot. In the country as a whole some two and a half million workers were on strike.

This, of course, left many times more people still at work: the small shop-keeper, the taxi driver, the cinema usher, the waiter, whatever their feelings about the merits or demerits of the general strike, did not feel that it related to them. From the point of view of the government this was clearly something to be welcomed, but at the same time it posed an almost insuperable problem. If they were to remain employed these people had to get to their place of work, yet the public transport on which they depended had largely ceased to operate. Those with cars for the most part took to the road and crammed into their vehicles as many would-be workers as they could accommodate: the result was traffic jams of epic density and, when trains or buses were operated by unskilled volunteers, a plethora of mishaps and minor accidents.

One of the most conspicuous victims of the strike was the national press. The printers were called out, leading to the disappearance of almost every newspaper, regardless of its political sympathies. Winston Churchill, more or less on his own initiative, took over the *Morning Post* and produced a strike-breaking news-sheet which he called the *British Gazette.* The B.B.C. kept going, doing its best to maintain a position of neutrality between strikers and non-strikers, but inevitably identified by those who resented its continued activity as a mouthpiece of the government.

In a way the most remarkable feature of the General Strike was the decorum with which it was conducted and the moderation shown by both sides in a situation which could easily have developed into a disastrous confrontation. The Oxford undergraduate who volunteered as a strike-breaking bus conductor might find his efforts provoked a certain amount of derision and occasional hostility, but none of them was lynched; equally, the strikers who tried to disrupt the efforts of those who were keeping the wheels of public life turning were checked wherever possible but rarely arrested or prosecuted. The offices of *The Times* were set ablaze, but this was an isolated instance and was deplored almost as vociferously by the strikers' leadership as by the employers. More typical was the much publicised match between the strikers and the police on the football ground at Plymouth. Ten thousand people watched a game in which the Chief Constable's wife kicked off and the police tactfully lost by two goals to one. Business was business, the event seemed to proclaim, but in the last resort there were other, still more important considerations. We were all British, and the tolerance and decency of the people would outlive any bitterness that the strike might bring.

How long this tolerance would have lasted is another matter. Undoubtedly, as the strike wore on, tempers were becoming frayed, bitterness mounted. There were more instances of violence recorded on the fourth and fifth days of the strike than on the first or second. On the whole, though, discipline prevailed. So far as the government and employers were concerned, this restraint was made more palatable by the feeling that things were moving their way. From the outset of the conflict it had been the preoccupation of the government to isolate the miners and to draw a distinction between them and the rank and file of the T.U.C. If the other unions could be persuaded, could even be led to suspect, that they were being required to sacrifice themselves to satisfy the unreasonable demands of one of their number, then the battle would be, if not wholly, then at least half won.

Distressingly soon – from the point of view, at least, of those who had the unity of the working classes at heart – it became clear that the Trades Union leaders were indeed increasingly ready to question the need to sacrifice themselves for the sake of the miners. Union funds were running low and enough blacklegs were breaking ranks and accepting employment to make the prospect of victory seem ever more remote. After five days, Stanley Baldwin, who till then had thought it best to keep a low profile, judged that the time had come to intervene. He spoke to the nation in terms of striking moderation; distinguishing between the action of the miners – which, though ill-advised, was a legitimate use of trades-union power – and the general strike, which was unconstitutional – "a direct attack on the community" by an unelected body which had not even bothered to consult its own membership before plunging the nation into industrial and financial chaos. He was the perfect man for the occasion: understated, studiously moderate, conspicuously (and probably sincerely) ready to concede that the workers had real grievances and that these must be righted once the strike was over.

First, though, the strike must end. The employers, Baldwin maintained, could not be expected to negotiate under duress. Fortunately for him, the solidarity of the strikers was already crumbling. By the end of the first week more trains and buses were coming back into operation every day: partly through the exertions of amateur strike-breakers who, sometimes with calamitous results, were prepared to have a go at filling the gap; more seriously, through the return of the strikers themselves, who had little stomach for a fight about which they had been dubious from the start and which they felt there was little hope of winning. They did not always find that the return to work was easy: some employers were in a vengeful mood and made difficulties over re-employing workers who they felt had been too quick to walk out or who had been instrumental in persuading others to do the same.

The resolution, or obduracy, of the miners remained the factor that kept the strike going. The fact was that they had less to lose than most of their fellow workers, and were prepared to put up with privations that their colleagues felt to be intolerable. Their determination brought their colleagues on the T.U.C. to something near despair. The Chairman of the General Council, Arthur Pugh, stated the situation with gloomy clarity. If the miners would not agree to negotiate after a return to work then the Trades Union movement as a whole was doomed to stand by them: like it or not the struggle must continue until "the process of attrition has brought the whole trade union movement to its knees".

It is hard to fix the precise moment at which the T.U.C. suffered a change of heart. Probably it was late on the night of Tuesday, 11 May, when the miners finally rejected a compromise that the Trades Union movement as a whole thought acceptable, even generous. "I wonder how long we are going to grovel on our hands and knees to the miners?" asked Pugh. Not for long, turned out to be his answer. The government, scenting victory and feeling that the national mood was behind them, made overt, even ostentatious preparations for battle, with troops massing at Wellington Barracks and armoured cars rolling down Oxford Street. It seems unlikely that Baldwin ever imagined that he would have recourse to arms – certainly the Trades Union leadership never gave him serious grounds to believe that it would be necessary – but a conspicuous demonstration of the government's resolve to react forcibly if they thought it necessary was both reassuring for the employers and a deterrent to the T.U.C. When the T.U.C. delegation, led by J. H. Thomas, went to Number Ten late in the morning of 12 May, it was in effect to surrender. The Prime Minister will only receive you if the strike has been called off, Sir Horace Wilson told them. We have come to call the strike off, replied Thomas.

The T.U.C. did their best to conceal the completeness of their defeat. The prime object of their efforts had been to ensure that the miners got a fair, or at least a better deal; they professed to be satisfied that this had now been achieved. Baldwin was happy to let them nurture this comforting illusion; he was at pains to look to the future rather than gloat over the past. "We should resume our work in the spirit of co-operation," he declared, "putting behind us all malice and all vindictiveness." King George V, who had at one time been in near despair at what seemed to him the intransigence of the strikers and the bloody-mindedness of the employers, struck the same note. "Let us forget whatever elements of bitterness the events of the last few days may have created," he pleaded in a message to his people, "only remembering how steady and orderly the country has remained, though severely tested, and forthwith address ourselves to the task of bringing into being a peace which will be lasting because, forgetting the past, it looks only to the future with the hopefulness of a united people."

His diary shows the extent of his relief. Even though the country had been dangerously divided and four million men had been called out on strike, not a shot had been fired, there had been little violence. "It shows what a wonderful people we are," he commented. Perhaps his conclusion was a little too complacent – "wonderful" is a strong word – but certainly the British, both employers and employed, had showed remarkable restraint and had seemed ready to accept that the national interest should be allowed to weigh at least as heavily in the balance as any consideration of personal gain. The General Strike was not something in which the British people could take inordinate pride, but certainly it was not something of which they needed to feel ashamed.

NOTES FOR FURTHER READING

For this chapter I have relied heavily on Anne Perkins's lucid and intelligent *A Very British Strike* (London 2006). Keith Laybourn's *The General Strike of 1926* (London 1993) and Margaret Morris and Jeffrey Skelley's *The General Strike 1926* (London 1976) are earlier studies of the same subject.

8

PENICILLIN

1928

In early September 1928 Alexander Fleming returned from holiday to resume his work in the laboratory of St Mary's Hospital in London's Paddington. He began to sort out the pile of culture plates that had accumulated during his absence. "That's funny!" he remarked, as he picked up a plate at random. It was funny. He had discovered penicillin.

This is, of course, hardly adequate as a description of a process of research that had already lasted for years and would go on for many more. It is not wholly absurd, however. There was a moment of dramatic revelation. It did lead directly to the discovery of penicillin. And the history of medicine, the history of the world indeed, was affected radically as a result.

* * *

Nobody who observed the childhood of Alec Fleming would have been likely to predict that he would one day become a scientific colossus of worldwide renown. He was the eighth child by a second wife of an Ayrshire farmer who leased his land from the Earl of Loudoun. There was always plenty to eat and enough warm clothing, even after his father died when Alec was still a

Alexander Fleming in his laboratory.

child, but the family operated at subsistence level and the boy had to walk four miles every day to get to the local school. He expected that, with his fifteenth birthday, he would join his eldest brother and start work on the farm, but he had shown himself to be an able scholar and a hard worker and the rest of the family concluded that it was worth sending him to the Academy at Kilmarnock. Meanwhile, three other of his brothers had found their way to London and, when still only thirteen, Alec joined them and began to attend lectures at the Polytechnic School in Regent Street. By the age of sixteen he had joined a shipping company, the American Line, earning a derisory wage but quickly establishing himself as totally reliable.

In 1900 the Boer War disturbed his progress. Alec volunteered and joined the London Scottish regiment. He never got to South Africa, but in the course of his training he showed himself to be an outstanding shot and made a name for himself at Bisley. Quite apart from the satisfaction of being a success, he considered his hours on the rifle range to have been time well spent. "There is far more in medicine than mere book-work," he told an audience of medical students many years later. "You have to know men and you have to know human nature. There is no better way to learn about human nature than by indulging in sports, more especially in team sports . . . Play games, and you will be able to read your books with a greater understanding of your patients." Whether those responsible for his audience's education welcomed Fleming's advocacy of team sports as a desirable element in higher education may be open to some doubt: not many students were able to devote much time to games and yet, like Fleming, pass every examination with triumphant ease. Fleming had no difficulty, however. From the moment at which he decided to abandon shipping and take to medicine, his climb to the summit of his new career seemed as effortless as it was inevitable. He passed top into St Mary's Hospital, in his first year won the Hospital Entrance Scholarship as well as the Chemistry and Biology Prizes, in his second and third year added the Physiology Prize, the Histology Prize and the Senior Anatomy Prize. At that point he planned to become a surgeon but he was persuaded instead to study bacteriology – partly, at least, because the St Mary's shooting team had need of his talents and it was realised that, if he took to surgery, he would be lost to the hospital.

It was a decision that shaped his life. In the Inoculation Department he found himself working under Almroth Wright, the recently appointed Professor of Pathology. Wright was a scholar of formidable ability and limitless ambitions. When still absurdly young he had done important work in a wide range of fields and was then offered a chair at the Army Medical School at Netley Hospital. At first he specialised in the mysteries of blood-clotting, then expanded into the field of bacteriology. But as well as being a scientist of real importance, Wright was arrogant and instinctively controversial. He did not suffer fools gladly, thought that almost all his colleagues were, if not actually fools, then at least by far his intellectual inferiors, and made his opinion embarrassingly clear. Not surprisingly he was little liked by his peers; his disciples on the other hand, those young men whom he had thought worth nurturing, revered and would have died for him. Fleming was one of these, yet he was also among the very few who dared from time to time to question or even contradict his master. Wright, who took his work with immense seriousness, accepted such criticism with some surprise but apparent calm. He was, however, disconcerted by the obvious relish with which Fleming pursued his studies. To enjoy one's work so heartily seemed almost frivolous: "You treat research like a game!" he once complained. Game or no game, he never doubted that he was nurturing a talent that would one day produce work of real significance. Early confirmation came in 1919 when Fleming was selected to deliver the Hunterian Lecture, an honour traditionally awarded to one who was not merely up and coming but had almost come. His subject was antiseptics and his tone was sceptical – antiseptics, he argued, might prevent infection but they were powerless to cure an infection once it had been established. He little imagined at the time that he, more than any other individual, was destined to put this right.

Nor would those who knew him best have thought that he was likely to introduce any startling innovation. For all his brilliance, Fleming was curiously unimaginative and prone to eschew any intellectual adventures. A friend once tried to persuade him of the importance of the unconscious mind. "What's the use of talking about the unconscious mind?" Fleming demanded. "There's no such thing! If you are unconscious you don't have a mind." What he wanted was facts: what he could not see was, if not irrelevant, then at least something that could safely be ignored. But he saw a great deal more than most people: his eyes were "large, observant, penetrating", his perceptions phenomenally acute. Not many scientists, when suffering from an acute attack of catarrh, would have been sufficiently curious to preserve and analyse their own nasal excretions; yet from this stemmed his first important breakthrough, the discovery of a new microbe – lysozyme – which possessed what seemed almost miraculous powers in defending the body against infections. Human tears, it turned out, were a prime source of this substance: for months to come friends and relations found themselves by one means or another reduced to tears so as to provide material for Fleming's researches. He was convinced that he had made a discovery of potentially vast significance; his peers, however, were un-enthused. When Fleming read a paper describing his work to the Medical Research Club he was met by dispiriting indifference. When, at the end of his presentation, the Chairman called for questions, not a word was said. Fleming – who, it is only fair to say, was a poor lecturer and gave his audience little reason to believe that they were hearing something of signal importance – was left standing on the platform amid almost total silence and eventually returned in some embarrassment to his seat to listen to the next paper.

* * *

He was undiscomfited. He felt that he was advancing towards a goal of vast significance and that one day the world would accept what he was doing; till then let them rest in ignorance. Once again a stroke of luck helped him on his way. Luck, of course, is likely to be a contributory element in almost every scientific breakthrough, but luck by itself is worth nothing unless it is supported by experience and an eye perceptive enough to recognise what it is looking at. Other scientists might have had a laboratory filled with dishes containing colonies of staphylococci; it took Fleming to observe that in one of them something unexpected was occurring. He picked up a dish and examined it quizzically. As was by no means unusual the culture had provoked a growth of mould, but in this case the colony of staphylococci had been dissolved. "That's funny!" said Fleming, picking off a scrap of the mould and carefully preserving it.

"What struck me," recorded a colleague who was present on the occasion, "was that he didn't confine himself to observing, but took action at once. Lots of people observe a phenomenon, feeling that it may be important, but they don't get beyond being surprised – after which they forget. That was never the case with Fleming."

But though, in hindsight, the discovery seems dramatic, it appeared of little moment at the time. Even Fleming, though he carefully preserved the mysterious mould, was in no great hurry to examine it. It was two months before he had conducted any serious experiments, another six before he had established to his own satisfaction that he had stumbled on a substance that could dissolve some of the most virulent of germs. Among these were those responsible for some of the diseases which had plagued humanity most persistently: pneumonia, meningitis, diptheria, syphilis, gonorrhoea. Always he insisted that he had not "invented" penicillin: he had merely identified it and given it its name. Even that last took some time. It was not till February 1929 that Fleming asked a mycologist friend, Professor La Touche, to identify the mould. La Touche was anxious not to be too precise but eventually concluded that it approximated to *Penicillium rubrum*. In fact he had got it wrong but, by the time the mistake was discovered, the christening had taken place. Penicillin it was and penicillin it would remain.

Given what we know today about the qualities of penicillin and what Fleming in 1929 must have suspected was its potential, it is hard to understand why the pace of development was so slow. In June 1929, in the *British Journal of Experimental Pathology,* he published a paper summarising his work to date. "It is suggested," the author stated boldly, "that it [penicillin] may be an efficient antiseptic for application to, or injection into, areas invaded by penicillin-sensitive microbes." Given the range and the potency of those microbes it was obvious that, if his claims were justified, the history of medicine would be transformed. Yet nobody seems to have paid much attention. Even as late as 1936, when Fleming once again expounded his theories at the Second International Congress of Microbiology, he was, if not ignored, at least given only a cursory hearing. "I spoke of penicillin in 1936," he later commented ruefully, "but I was lacking in eloquence and nobody took any notice." He *was* lacking in eloquence, yet the substance of what he said should surely have impressed at least some members of his audience. On the contrary: "It's just old Fleming again on his usual hobby-horse" was the stock reaction. Even he seems to some extent to have lost interest if not belief in his own discovery: its usefulness, he began to believe, was limited; the problems involved in its supply and application seemed impossible to overcome. He used it in a few cases with excellent results but, in his own words, "in peacetime septic wounds are uncommon in hospital and, as the potency of penicillin rapidly disappears on keeping, the therapeutic aspect of this substance was dropped". Even when the magnitude of his achievement had been recognised and he had become the best-known scientist in the land, a trace of scepticism remained. "I don't think my work on penicillin is the best I've ever done," he once remarked, "but it is the one that got into the papers."

Though his initial contribution had been of inestimable importance, the reason that it finally got into the papers was largely the doing of Howard Florey. Florey was an Australian who, in 1929, had begun to take an interest in the work that Fleming was doing in the field of lysozymes and who carried on that work when he was appointed to the Chair of Pathology at Oxford. By the summer of 1940, when the British Army was evacuated from Dunkirk and the Battle of Britain was raging overhead, work in the laboratory had reached a critical point. Fifty white mice were given what should have been a lethal injection of virulent streptococci. Twenty-five were then treated with penicillin. Within sixteen hours the twenty-five mice which had not been given penicillin were all dead; of the twenty-five that had been treated, twenty-four survived. Penicillin worked.

"One can," wrote the Nobel Prize-winning physician, Macfarlane Burnet, "think of the middle of the twentieth century as the end of one of the perhaps most important social revolutions in history – the virtual elimination of infectious disease as a significant factor in social life." "Perhaps" is one of the more important words in that declaration, and penicillin was, of course, not the only factor in what was undoubtedly a dramatic transformation of the public health. But the discovery of penicillin was without question the single most important breakthrough in that era of explosive advance. Not merely were its results dramatic in their own right, they opened the way for the surgeon to undertake a plethora of complex and perilous operations which he would not have dared attempt in an earlier age. Significant though the contribution made by other people might have been, it is Fleming to whom the greatest credit must be given.

It took some time for his achievement to be fully acknowledged. "The man of genius is often an egotist," wrote Lord Beaverbrook – the subject of egotism being one on which he was well qualified to speak with authority. "When, as sometimes happens, he is simple and retiring, the world is inclined to underestimate his gifts. Sir Alexander Fleming was a genius of this rare type." But in the end fame caught up with him. By the end of the war penicillin had become an indispensable part of the medical process, saving tens of thousands, probably hundreds of thousands of lives that would otherwise have been lost. And the word "penicillin" became inextricably associated in the public mind with the name of Fleming.

Perhaps, indeed, this was carried too far: Florey and his colleagues were entitled to feel a little disgruntled at the scant attention paid to their monumental contribution. But the world wanted one identifiable hero and no-one could say that Fleming did not deserve his honours. He and his "miracle drug" became household names: he became a Fellow of the Royal Society – the ultimate accolade of British science – in 1943; he was awarded a knighthood and a plethora of prizes and other honours in 1944; shared the Nobel Prize with Florey and Florey's colleague, Ernst Chain, in 1945. He was the best-known living scientist in the world, glittering in an empyrean with fellow superstars like Newton or Pasteur. He enjoyed his glory but never lost his sense of proportion or his sense of humour. He would have relished the story of Mrs Margaret Goldsmith who visited an exhibition devoted to penicillin at St Mary's Hospital. As she approached the entrance to the exhibition the Secretary of the Hospital pointed to a closed door and said in an awestruck tone: "In that room Professor Fleming discovered penicillin!" There was a white card pinned to the door and Mrs Goldsmith bent forward to see what it said. It read: "Cat in residence."

NOTES FOR FURTHER READING

There are many biographies of Alexander Fleming. The most substantial is that by André Maurois, translated from the French by Gerard Hopkins (London 1959). More recent is Gwyn Macfarlane's *Alexander Fleming. The Man and the Myth* (London 1984). Robert Bud's *Penicillin. Triumph and Tragedy* (Oxford 2007) is the best study of the subject for the general reader.

9

"THE BROADWAY MELODY"

1929

On 8 February, 1929 "The Broadway Melody" was shown publicly for the first time. Its venue was the Astor Theatre in New York. It was the first musical film to be made partly in Technicolor, the first musical to be made by Metro-Goldwyn-Mayer – M.G.M. – and the first all-talking musical made in Hollywood. It thus introduced what was arguably to be the United States' greatest contribution to twentieth-century culture. By most other standards it was, if not a disaster, then at least decidedly inglorious.

* * *

Nothing sensational had happened in the first half of the 1920s in the world of American cinema. The romance and marriage of Mary Pickford and Douglas Fairbanks commanded more headlines than any single film, though in Charlie Chaplin's "The Kid", introducing the six-year-old Jackie Coogan, the silent cinema achieved something close to its apotheosis. Then, in 1927, came Al Jolson in "The Jazz Singer", the first full-length talking film, and almost overnight it became clear that, whatever its artistic merits might be, the public was no longer going to be content with the silent film. Ramon Navarro, Buster Keaton,

Anita Page, Charles King and Bessie Love flanked by the chorus girls
of "The Broadway Melody"

Gloria Swanson, all great artists and stars of worldwide fame, accepted with varying degrees of grace that their day was done and disappeared from the scene. John Gilbert was perhaps the most conspicuous casualty. He was the ultimate great romantic hero of the silent screen, a star whose profile had won the hearts of innumerable susceptible women. Now Gilbert spoke, and it became painfully apparent that his voice was nothing like as sexy as his profile. Almost overnight he was transformed, if not into a figure of fun, then at least into a miserable shadow of the public idol which he had so recently been.

For the film industry based in Hollywood the advent of sound represented, in the long term, a vista of infinite possibilities. In the short term it meant disaster. At first only a handful of cinemas were equipped to handle the new technology. The owners and managers of cinemas showing silent films told themselves hopefully that, while the public might be briefly dazzled by the novelty set before them, they would not for that reason lose their taste for more traditional fare. To their dismay they found that their cinemas were deserted; the audiences which had filled the halls of every provincial town now flocked to the cities in search of halls where they could be sure of discovering a more fulfilling experience.

Demand, as it usually does, created supply. Within a remarkably short period all the major studios had largely, if not entirely, switched over to sound. M.G.M. were one of the leaders. In this they showed themselves adventurous but, when it came to the choice of film they, unsurprisingly, played safe. Romance, they knew, was a sure-fire hit; so was comedy. Romantic comedy, therefore, was the zone to aim for; and it would be still more sure to gain popularity if a certain amount of song and dance was thrown in. Irving Thalberg, M.G.M.'s production supremo and one of the most powerful men in Hollywood, decided to work to this prescription. If a film was set in theatreland it would be easier to introduce the musical element without calling for too much ingenuity on the part of the script writers. Broadway would, therefore, be an ideal venue. Men in white tie and tails; women, lots of women, in almost no clothes at all; dialogue of dire predictability; a clutter of unambitious but tolerably hummable tunes: it was a formula that was to dominate Hollywood for the next thirty years or so and, incidentally, in the hands of a genius like Fred Astaire, produce a handful of the most daringly conceived and skilfully executed works of art in cinema.

"The Broadway Melody" can, alas, not be included in this select category, but it wasn't too bad. The plot, though exiguous, made sense and provided an adequate vehicle for the four stars who had to be given something to do for most of the two hours or so that the entertainment lasted. Harriet – "Hak" – and Queenie Mahoney, two sisters who performed a vaudeville act in the provinces, venture to New York to try their luck on Broadway. Eddie Kearns, the impresario who has brought the sisters to New York, tries to secure them parts in a new revue – "The Broadway Melody". Eddie is engaged to Hak but falls in love with Queenie. Queenie, who secretly returns his love but is concerned for the happiness of her sister, instead has an affair with an unscrupulous playboy called Jock. Everyone misunderstands everyone else, most people end up with the wrong partner and nobody lives happily ever after. A good time is had by all.

It is hard to understand today how this musical, at the best modestly inoffensive, can have achieved the success it did, making more money than any other film that year and yielding M.G.M. a profit of $1.6 million. Partly, the explanation of the enormous haul is that the film was remarkably cheap to make. "We don't know whether the audience will accept a musical on film," remarked Irving Thalberg when work was just beginning, "so we'll have to shoot it as fast and cheaply as we can." The original budget had been $500,000, and while most heads of production would have sought excuses to exceed it, Thalberg spent even less. The movie was shot with a single camera bolted to the floor, operated from a steamy and enclosed booth, yet somehow contrived to give the impression that no expense had been spared. His reward was a production that became a by-word for lavish extravagance. "The Broadway Melody" was nominated for three Oscars and won the Academy Award for Best Picture. It inspired three successors – different in many ways but recognisably from the same stable – "Broadway Melody of 1936", "Broadway Melody of 1938" and "Broadway Melody of 1940". There would have been a "Broadway Melody of 1944" but M.G.M. for some reason lost heart and settled for "Broadway Rhythm". The main reason for its phenomenal success is surely that there was no competition: the fact that "The Broadway Melody" has been made to look thin and meretricious in comparison with other films in the same genre makes one forget that when it came out there was no film with which it could reasonably be compared. "This picture is great. It will revolutionise the talkies," wrote Edwin Schallert in *Motion Picture News*. "The direction is an amazing indication of what can be done in the new medium." It quickly proved to be an indication of what *would* be done in the new medium. The importance of "The Broadway Melody" is that it introduced singing and dancing to the cinema; the fact that neither the singing nor the dancing were of the highest order is relatively unimportant.

Not that the production was as bad as all that. The film would not have succeeded if it had not been for performances of considerable competence by several major stars. Anita Page, who played the part of Queenie Mahoney, though still only nineteen at the time, had already earned a formidable reputation, having the previous year played opposite Joan Crawford in "Our Dancing Daughters". Anyone who was involved romantically with Clark Gable and propositioned by Benito Mussolini commands a certain respect, but Page was perhaps most celebrated for retiring at the age of twenty-four and then re-emerging sixty years later to appear in several low-budget horror films. It cannot be said that her reputation was thereby enhanced but the effort was commendable. She died aged ninety-three, the last survivor of those who attended the first Academy Awards in 1929.

Bessie Love, who played Hak, was nominated for Best Actress in those Awards, losing with honour to no less a star than Mary Pickford. Unlike Anita Page she had made her name in the silent films and was one of the few who sucessfully made the leap to sound. The fact that she had followed this course was very obvious: to the modern eye, at least, she over-acts ferociously, her face conveying anger, grief or love with an intensity that suggests she had no voice at her disposal with which to convey the same emotions. Contemporaries did not agree: as well as being nominated for an Oscar she was the only member of the cast approved unequivocally by Mordaunt Hill who, in a cautiously critical review in the *New York Times*, found the film over-sentimental and "rather obvious" but thought that Love was "capital in either her tempestuous or tearful periods".

Eddie Kearns was played by Charles King: a competent performance but one which any devotee of Westerns would find sadly out of character. King is known above all as the villain of innumerable Wild West romances; it is said that no man was killed more regularly by John Wayne. The director, Harry Beaumont, was as distinguished as any of the stars. In the days of silent films he had directed John Barrymore in "Beau Brummel" and Joan Crawford in "Our Dancing Daughters"; he came to terms with sound but never quite recaptured the glories of his youth.

NOTES FOR FURTHER READING

The reviews of "The Broadway Melody" in the American and British press provide the main source for this chapter. Lucy Fischer's *American Cinema of the 1920s* (Rutgers University Press 2009) and Emanuel Levy's *All About Oscar. The History and Politics of the Academy Awards* (New York 2003) provide useful background.

10

THE WALL STREET CRASH

1929

Tuesday, 29 October, 1929, was the most catastrophic single day in a disastrous season. From the moment the market opened panic-stricken selling began. By the end of the day, in spite of a tentative and, as it turned out, ephemeral rally in the late afternoon, more than sixteen million sales had been recorded: losses were so great that all the gains of the previous year had been wiped out. Things, in fact, were even worse than they appeared: so overwhelming was the Niagara of sales that large batches of selling orders were put to one side, slipped from view, and were only discovered after the markets had closed and the dealers were ruefully coming to terms with the scale of the collapse. More shares changed hands on "Bloody Tuesday" than in any normal three-month period. It was the day that, more than any other, epitomised the "Wall Street Crash".

* * *

It was, of course, more a case of the "Wall Street Crashes", or, since any crash is normally presaged by a boom, the "Wall Street Booms"; and boom and crash were made inevitable not by, or not primarily by, economic circumstances but by human aspirations. Those aspirations were voiced most starkly by John Raskob, a

An unfortunate investor tries to sell his car. The placard reads: "$100 will buy this car must have cash lost all on the stock market."

tycoon who played a leading role in both General Motors and DuPont and who, in the late summer of 1929, gave an interview to the *Ladies' Home Journal* which appeared under the headline "Everybody ought to be rich". Not merely *ought* they to be rich, Raskob contended, but, with only a modest effort on their part, they *could* be rich. It was the destiny of the United States to grow ever more prosperous; no more recessions, no more boom and bust, just steady growth and an ever more comfortable style of living. He was telling the American people not merely what they wanted to hear but what they believed to be true. Guaranteed employment, rising property values, ever increasing wages: these were the outward and visible signs of a steadily growing economy.

More than any of these, however, the Americans had grown to associate the wealth of the nation and their own individual well-being with the movement of stocks and shares on the New York Stock Exchange. Despite the occasional setback, the 1920s had seen sensational growth on Wall Street. The Americans had watched with ever-increasing fascination as the activities of the brokers moved from the financial pages of the newspapers to those sections traditionally reserved for wars, plagues and sport. Playing the stock market had indeed become a national sport: even those who had no broker and had never owned a share took note of the sensational rise in value of the great American companies and mused upon the riches that might have been theirs if only they had had the money and the acumen to enter the market. "The striking thing about the stock-market speculation of 1929," wrote that economic guru, J. K. Galbraith, "was not the massiveness of the participation. Rather it was the way it became central to the culture."

Everyone with even a glimmering of interest in such matters followed with fascinated excitement the boom of the 1920s. Almost everyone assumed that it was bound to go on and on. There were a handful of sceptics. "Do you still feel as I do?" the Governor of New York, a certain Franklin Delano Roosevelt, enquired of a friend, "that there may be a limit to the increase of security values?" Most investors, however, saw no reason to believe that such a limit existed. There would probably be a slowing-up in the pace of growth, conceivably even there might be a pause in which the market could regain its breath, but upwards, ever upwards, must be the way forward for Wall Street. It was not just the investors and the brokers who took so rosy a view of the financial future. Calvin Coolidge, President of the United States from 1923 to 1929, saw it as his duty to stoke the fires of the booming market rather than to try to abate the flames. "The business of America is business," Coolidge had famously observed a few months after taking office, and the business of the President of the United States was to give business its head and utter encouraging noises from the side-lines. Herbert Hoover, his successor, was rather more alive to the perils of the situation but, when it came to the point, made no serious or sustained effort to impose sobriety. "The fundamental business of the country . . . is on a sound and prosperous basis," he proclaimed hopefully in October 1929; whether he believed it or not, these were not the words of a man disposed to pour cold water on the waxing flames. Himself a self-made millionaire, he was satisfied that it was within the powers of any hard-working and sensible American to win himself, if not millions, then at least a comfortable livelihood. "The poorhouse is vanishing from among us," he had trumpeted on the campaign trail. "We shall soon, with the help of God, be in sight of the day when poverty will be banished from this earth." "This earth", presumably, encompassed only the United States of America, but, even so, it was an ambitious undertaking.

Hoover was not wholly blind to the perils of an uncontrolled and perhaps uncontrollable boom, but even though he might perceive the need for restraint he lacked the weapons to enforce it. What should have been the most formidable instrument at his disposal was the Federal Reserve Board in Washington. It signally failed to play its part; indeed, it was itself a major contributor to the explosive boom. Early in 1927, responding to the pleas of the hard-pressed European bankers, the New York Federal Reserve Bank had cut its rediscount rate and thus poured money onto the market. "From that date," concluded Lionel Robbins of the London School of Economics, "according to all the evidence, the situation got completely out of control." In February 1929 the Bank took fright and proposed that the rediscount rate should be restored to its level of 1926 or even raised still higher. The Reserve Board in Washington shrank from taking a step which would have inconvenienced a multitude of speculators and been resented by a public which had been taught to believe that growth was sacred and large profits inevitable. It dithered and procrastinated; when it finally got round to raising the rediscount rate it was by too little and done too late. Even these timid measures, however, were denounced by the apostles of growth. "There are two things that can disrupt business in this country," said the cowboy comedian, Will Rogers. "One is war and the other is a meeting of the Federal Reserve Bank." The Bank knew that it was unpopular, dreaded being more so, and as a result failed to do its duty.

Claud Cockburn, the Anglo-Irish journalist who, a few years later, was to launch his own explosively intemperate newspaper, *The Week*, was in New York at the time. On Thursday, October 24 he was due to lunch with Sir Edgar Speyer, an immensely rich banker who had made his fortune in London and now lived in New York. He walked down Wall Street on his way to Speyer's house in Washington Square and was struck by the huge crowds milling around the financial areas, apparently aimless, saying little, just watching and waiting, as if in anticipation of some unpredictable but immensely significant event. At Speyer's house there seemed to be no such apprehension, all was calm and ordered. Then there was an uproar in the adjoining room, where the servants were gathered. A harassed butler asked Speyer to come through. The servants had been following the events in Wall Street on a ticker tape in the kitchen. All of them had a stake in the stock market – tiny, of course, by the standards of their employer but still more than they could afford to lose. What they had been listening to was the step-by-step development of a catastrophe, and every minute it seemed that the steps were becoming more ruinous, the catastrophe more complete. Speyer hurried away and was seen no more at home that day; the remaining guests got through lunch as best they could and then dispersed into a city that was becoming more demoralised by the minute. Trading on the stock exchange was closed at three o'clock but such was the volume of business, so ruinous had been the falls, that it was seven that evening before all the transactions had been recorded.

That was "Black Thursday"; it seemed at the time as if nothing could be worse but it was only a presage of what was to come. In a sense American investors should by now have been inured to the possibility of things going wrong; there had been sharp falls on the market as well as rises over the previous few months and fortunes had been lost as well as made. The underlying assumption, however, remained that, in the long run, things could only get better: the government was stable, the economy was sound, all must be well. On October 24, investors for the first time realised that the ice on which they had been skating was perilously thin. Now it was cracking; if it disintegrated they would find themselves in the water; the water was cold and deep and they were not sure that they knew how to swim.

Panic followed. Wall Street had never witnessed such scenes before. Under the pressure of events even the most sacred rules of propriety were abandoned. Traders on the stock exchange were traditionally forbidden to "run, curse, push or go coatless". On October 24, men in shirt sleeves were running anxiously from here to there and back again: why they were doing so they had no clear idea, but at least if they moved fast enough they could delude themselves that they were in some way keeping up with events. In that one day some thirteen million shares were traded, far more than on any previous day in the history of Wall Street. Throughout the financial district firms worked all night to try to catch up with events and to face the coming Friday in good order if with dire apprehension.

And then it seemed as if there had been no need for apprehension after all. On Friday and on Saturday morning prices remained generally steady; there were more falls than gains but the falls were relatively small, no more than might be expected on any normal working day. Wall Street licked its wounds and told itself that the worst was over. It had been given a sharp reminder that what went up was likely one day to go down, that pride went before a fall. It told itself that it had learnt its lesson. It would take time for the market to regain its peak but that it would do so within a few weeks or perhaps months was felt to be assured.

What happened over the weekend to destroy this confidence? Partly, perhaps, it was that a backlog of selling orders was left over from the week before so that the first thing brokers encountered on Monday was a sharp fall in the market. Partly, a multitude of small investors had had time to reflect on the events of the week before and had concluded that the stock market was not a proper place for them to be: better to get out while the going was still relatively good and invest what was left of their money in real estate, pictures, cars, anything that was tangible and might be expected to hold its value. At all events, fragile hopes quickly turned to apprehension, apprehension to fear, fear to panic. By 11 a.m. it was Black Thursday all over again. Fewer shares were traded than on Thursday – nine and a quarter million as opposed to thirteen million – but the losses were greater and the collapse in confidence more complete. The giants of the market conferred anxiously and concluded that there was nothing to be done; the Federal Reserve Bank conferred anxiously and concluded that there was nothing to be done; for the rest it was *sauve qui peut* and the devil take the hindmost.

And so it was Tuesday, 29 October, and the devil took not merely the hindmost but a large number of those who had fondly imagined themselves to be immune to the market's vagaries. From the moment that business began it was clear that this was going to be a day that would make even Black Thursday seem endurable. There appeared to be no limit to the quantity of stock, much of it in what had hitherto been considered as being among the bluest of blue chips, which dealers were prepared to throw onto the market, regardless of the price it made. In the first half-hour 630,000 shares changed hands. The Federal Reserve board met at 10 a.m. and remained in session till close of play, but it seemed no more capable of taking any decisive action than it had on previous days. Only when George L. Harrison, Governor of the New York Federal Reserve Bank, more or less on his own initiative took the decision to release a hundred million dollars in government securities so as to reinvigorate the money market, did it seem possible that total disaster might be averted. The tide was not turned but it was checked; gradually some semblance of order was restored.

It was too late to save some of the protagonists. The giants of Wall Street had been sadly mauled but most of them survived; many of the smaller fry were brutally extinguished. Popular legend has it that many of these found the destruction of their fortunes and their reputations unendurable and committed suicide, usually by jumping from a window. If one believed the more sensational reports, people walking down Wall Street were constantly having to step aside so as to avoid the shattered body of the latest victim. For the most part this is gory fantasy. The statistics show that the number of suicides was little greater in the weeks following the Great Crash than it had been at any other period. The sum total of human misery was, however, formidable. Millions of people were substantially poorer as a result of the Crash, thousands lost everything and worse. It was not just that their investments were worthless; often they had borrowed or bought on credit and now found that they were heavily in debt. A multitude of investors and their dependants were affected, most of whom had never set foot in Wall Street or even knew what a share certificate looked like. Harpo Marx, like his brother Groucho, had invested heavily and suffered accordingly. "I had scraped the bottom of the barrel," he wrote, "liquidated every asset I owned except my harp and my croquet set . . . borrowed as far in advance as I could against my salary. My market holdings . . . were probably worth a medium-sized bag of jelly beans."

* * *

A stock-market crash was one thing, a prolonged depression another. The second did not inevitably have to follow the first. There had been sharp falls in the market in the past but usually they had been followed by a gradual, sometimes even a rapid recovery. Most people assumed that this would be the case in 1930. The Federal Reserve, which had been so slow to act when the market was too high, proved readier to respond when the figures began to move the other way. In February 1930 it lowered the discount rate to 4 per cent. This surely would be enough? President Hoover certainly thought so. "Gentlemen, you have come sixty days too late. The depression is over," he assured a delegation from the National Unemployment League in mid-1930. *The Wall Street Journal* was equally confident. "The worst of the current industrial recession has passed," it proclaimed. "Stock prices have started on an upward trend of major proportions." Yet somehow the American investor did not accept these comfortable predictions and failed to respond as his betters thought he should. The high-spirited confidence that had reigned in the country at large was now utterly lacking; try as the optimists might it was to be many years before it was glad, confident morning again. The depression, whatever President Hoover might say or think, was far from over. Indeed, it had hardly begun.

It is hard to say why the optimists were proved so signally wrong. It is true that not all was healthy with the American economy in the months before the Crash: industrial activity had slowed down, production was nevertheless beginning to exceed demand, shop sales over the counter were proving worryingly weak. But the malaise appeared to be only skin-deep; the professionals believed that fundamentally the economy was strong and poised to recover. It was the individually less important yet far more numerous amateurs, the casual players of the market, who refused to be reassured. *The Wall Street Journal*, so recently the trumpeter of good tidings, now took fright at this inexplicable malaise. "Sentiment rules the market, and is about as low as it has been in a number of months," it admitted ruefully, some months after the worst of the crisis seemed theoretically to have passed. A sustained slump set in. Within eighteen months of the Wall Street Crash the total of unemployed had reached two million, before too long it would be twelve million, industrial stocks were worth only 20 percent of the value they had achieved at their peak. On

Wall Street, where recently brokers had watched in alarm as the volume of business grew hectically, there was now dismay when the number of shares traded dwindled by the day. And it seemed as if it were never going to stop. Prices on the stock market did not reach their nadir until the summer of 1932. President Roosevelt's New Deal with its three Rs – Relief for the unemployed and poor, Recovery of the economy to normal levels and Reform of the financial system so as to make sure that the same thing could not happen again – did something to turn the tide, but it took the Second World War fully to galvanise the economy and launch the United States on the road to full recovery.

The Great Crash of 1929 left a scar on the American psyche which was to last until all those who had been affected by it had left the scene. Even today it is not wholly forgotten. It should not be forgotten. It happened beause of an unfortunate conjuncture of economic factors but it happened too because of human greed and hubris. He would be a bold man who claimed that such factors were no longer to be met with today. There have been slumps and recessions since 1929 and there will be more in the future. So far, however, there has been nothing so catastrophically destructive, nothing, even the crash of 2008, which has laid waste so many lives. All those operating on the market today should be required by law to remind themselves at least once a year of what happened in 1929. Only if they bear those events in mind can one be reasonably sure that Bloody Tuesday will not come again.

NOTES FOR FURTHER READING

No one individual was so far responsible for the Crash as to make his biography essential reading. Of those concerned, President Hoover is probably most relevant. Gary Dean Best's *The Life of Herbert Hoover: Keeper of the Torch* (New York 2013) is one of the most recent and comprehensive biographies. Among the many general studies of the subject the most readable is that by J. K. Galbraith, *The Great Crash 1929* (London 1955). John Brooks's *Once in Golconda* (London 1970) and Maury Klein's *Rainbow's End* (Oxford 2001) are among the more recent studies.

11

GANDHI'S MARCH TO THE SEA

1930

Early in the morning of Sunday, 6 April, 1930, a slight, bald, super-ficially undistinguished man of sixty, wearing a clean but shabby dhoti, stepped onto the beach at Dandi, on the Bombay coastline, bathed briefly in the sea, then stooped and picked up a handful of salt from the beach. The salt was of low quality, mixed with sand and almost valueless. The gesture was worth an empire.

* * *

Of the handful of people who were aware of the birth of Mohan-das Karamchand Gandhi on 2 October, 1869 in the small coastal town of Porbandar, two hundred or so miles north of Bombay, none would have had any reason to believe that the future of India would be crucially affected by this event. "Mahatma", as Gandhi was habitually styled in later life, means "Great Soul", and who would have predicted that a great soul would spring from a well-established and modestly prosperous family – upper middle-class in British terms – who had served the dewan of Porbandar for several generations? Nor did the childish Gandhi seem in any way exceptional. His education, as was normal for boys of his class and generation, was mainly in English, but,

Gandhi and Sarojini Naidu, a politician, poet and independence activist known as "The Nightingale of India".

though he was clearly no fool, he did not shine at school and even failed one of the more important examinations. His family were orthodox Hindus and dutifully attended the appropriate temple, but Gandhi found little to attract or interest him in the religious services. "I did not like its glitter and pomp," he later confessed, and there is no reason to believe that he found much more to attract him in the substance that underlaid the glitter. He did not wholly eschew glitter and pomp, however, when it came to his own appearance. In 1888 he went for three years to London and kitted himself out at the Army and Navy Stores with a selection of suits that he felt suitable to his status. He seemed, as one of his compatriots noted disapprovingly, "a student more interested in fashion and frivolity than in his studies". This should not be made too much of. Gandhi was a diligent student who worked hard to qualify as a barrister. He lived frugally and never wavered in his vegetarian principles. There was no hint, however, that he was particularly concerned about racial issues or that he was likely to evolve into a crusader who would, more than any other individual, destroy the edifice of British India.

Popular legend attributes Gandhi's conversion to an incident in South Africa, the country in which he lived for the first fourteen years of his working life. He arrived in Durban, innocently bought a first-class ticket for the train to Pretoria, settled in his seat and was then ejected onto the platform at Maritzburg when a white fellow passenger complained to the conductor (another version of the story has it that the fellow passenger told the conductor that he had no objection to Gandhi's presence. "Oh, well, if you want to sit with a kaffir . . ." said the conductor disgustedly). It is not in the least improbable that such an incident occurred, but unlikely that Gandhi would have been surprised by this manifestation of a racial prejudice of which he must already have been well aware. His instinct was always to defy what he saw as the indefensible persecution of a coloured majority by a white minority: to seat himself in a carriage from which he knew he was likely to be ejected would have been entirely in accordance with that principle. (It is interesting that Gandhi was primarily, if not exclusively, preoccupied by the treatment of the Indian population of South Africa – he cannot have been blind to the sufferings of the native Africans but they do not seem to have bulked large in his mind.)

It was in South Africa that Gandhi evolved the doctrine of Satyagraha, passive resistance. Injustice must be combated, unfair and unreasonable laws should not be obeyed, but there must be no resort to violence: independence won at the price of human life, whoever's life it might be, was not worth having. "If we want freedom," Gandhi wrote, "we shall not gain it by killing or injuring others but by dying or submitting ourselves to suffering." It cannot be said that the lot of the Indian in South Africa when Gandhi finally left to return to India was significantly better than when he had first arrived but he had at least kindled an awareness in people's minds. A new age of liberalism had not dawned but many people of political importance, including, most significantly, General Smuts, the future Prime Minister, were now awake to racial problems in a way that they had not been before.

In South Africa Gandhi had learnt to associate British imperialism with racial prejudice and the exclusion of the indigenous inhabitants from any significant access to the machinery of power. The English-speakers might be somewhat less illiberal than the Boers but it was still a question of "them against us", with the British definitely being part of "them" against the coloured "us". The remarkable thing is that, when he landed at Bombay early in 1915, it was by no means as an inveterate enemy of the Empire. The British, he believed, had given a lot to India and had more to give. But there was also much about British rule which he condemned. "The British government in India," he wrote, "constitutes a struggle between the Modern Civilisation, which is the Kingdom of Satan, and the Ancient Civilisation, which is the Kingdom of God." It was the Kingdom of Satan which was to the fore in April 1919 when General Dyer at Amritsar ordered his troops to fire on a largely unarmed and peacefully intentioned crowd and left nearly four hundred dead. To add insult to this injury, for the next few weeks Indians were required to crawl on their hands and knees if they wished to pass the spot where Miss Sherwood, an English schoolteacher and missionary, had been attacked. Gandhi was even more disturbed by the crawling than he had been by the massacre; the former had only "destroyed a few bodies", the latter "tried to kill the soul of a nation". No single incident did more to forfeit the loyalty of those Indans still sympathetic to the Raj or to convince Gandhi that the campaign of Satyagraha must be relentlessly pursued.

The smartly suited and superficially Westernised Gandhi who had fitted in so well in London had now finally disappeared. Dress for Gandhi possessed a significance beyond the merely sartorial, not just because his dhoti, made from rough homespun cloth, symbolised his identification with the Indian masses, but because the cloth itself was something which, he felt, every

Indian could and should produce. To spin one's own cloth, for Gandhi, was to be self-reliant; it provided, in part at least, an answer to India's oppressive poverty; it gave the villager not merely something to wear but pride in his own achievement. Gandhi believed – not wholly without reason – that Britain had wilfully suppressed India's cottage industry so as to ensure a market for the cotton mills of Lancashire. This wrong must be redressed. His more sophisticated and worldly colleagues found his obsession with spinning faintly absurd. Nehru dutifully went through the motions of spinning a few yards of khadi but privately thought that it was a waste of time; cotton could be more cheaply and efficiently produced by modern machinery, why try to turn back the clock and condemn India to linger in a world of cottage industry? Economically he was no doubt right, but Gandhi was not and did not strive to be an economist. He was preoccupied not by the prosperity but by the pride, the spirit of the Indian peasant. Both men had a valid truth, but Gandhi's truth was perhaps the more fundamental.

* * *

The British never quite knew what to make of Gandhi. Churchill dismissed him as a "seditious fakir" and deplored the fact that he was received at Viceroy's House, but that was in 1931 and even Churchill would in the end have admitted that the Mahatma was a far more formidable figure than he had first appeared. In a way that was surprising to his compatriots and inexplicable to the British, Gandhi combined the ideals and the asceticism of a saint with the cunning of a successful and unscrupulous lawyer. The fact that he was committed to non-violence led the British to believe that he was, relatively speaking, a safe man, to be preferred to his more overtly seditious colleagues; in fact, as they subsequently realised, he did far more to undermine the British Raj than any number of the more belligerent members of the Congress Party.

Gandhi set out his views with striking clarity in a letter to the Viceroy, Lord Irwin, later Earl of Halifax. "Dear Friend", he began – a form of address that the sternly formal Viceroy could hardly have relished. He held British rule in India to be a curse, he wrote, but did not consider Englishmen in general to be worse than any other people on earth. Nevertheless, the British had "impoverished the dumb millions by a system of progressive exploitation and by a ruinously expensive military and civil administration". The Viceroy himself, to take only the most conspicuous example, was paid 700 rupees a day, five thousand times more than the average Indian wage. The taxes which the British levied were more than the Indian could bear – "The British system seems to be designed to crush the very life out of him." Worst of all was the tax on salt. It was from this time that Gandhi increasingly concentrated his efforts on securing the abolition, or at least the reduction of the salt tax, which he saw as being a heartless imposition on those least able to bear it. "The tax shows itself still more burdensome on the poor man when it is remembered that salt is the one thing he must eat more than the rich man . . . It saps the foundation both of their health and morals." Salt, like cloth, was something that the peasant could see, could touch, could understand. Freedom from foreign rule, free speech, the right to vote, were admirable concepts, to be fought for and, if necessary, to die for; but Gandhi was realistic enough to know that to most Indians they were just vague words that had no real relevance to their daily life. Salt was part of that life.

The coasts of India were rich in salt. Theoretically it was illegal for anyone except an authorised dealer to gather it; in practice the British knew that it was impossible to police even a small part of this vast area; they contented themselves with deterring would-be offenders by occasional prosecutions. Otherwise, they turned a blind eye to what was going on. They knew that the casual depredations of illicit salt-collectors would supply only a tiny part of India's needs; the salt tax made up an important part of the national revenue and, provided that contribution did not fall substantially, they were not going to worry about trivial infringements of the law. Open defiance was another matter: it threatened not merely the national revenues but the very authority of the state. If Gandhi had surreptitiously gleaned a few handfuls of salt from the beaches near Bombay nobody would have been concerned; when he chose to do so in open defiance of the law and with a maximum of publicity, the threat to the British Raj became patent and significant.

And so he conceived the project of the Salt March. First he wrote to the Viceroy and announced his intention of publicly and ostentatiously defying the law. Lord Irwin confined himself to polite regrets that Gandhi was proposing to act in a way that would inevitably disturb the public peace. Since disturbing the public peace was precisely what Gandhi was intending, this warning only encouraged him in his resolution. "I repudiate the law," he announced. And so, in the early morning of 12 March,

1930, Gandhi set out with a small band of his followers to walk the two hundred and forty miles to the little town of Dandi, on the shore of the Arabian sea. He took it for granted that he would quickly be arrested and that his martyrdom would stir the Indian masses as nothing else could have done. The authorities, however, elected not to oblige him. Whatever his intentions might be, he had as yet done nothing wrong. Let him walk to his heart's content; only when he was in overt breach of the law would they intervene. Even then they would be in no particular hurry to gratify his wish to cause a stir.

Gandhi started his march accompanied by eighty or so companions, chosen for their physical fitness, their loyalty and, most of all, their self-discipline. From time to time supporters from the villages along the way joined the march but they were not encouraged to come too far; Gandhi had no wish to build up a cavalcade that the authorities might find threatening and the problem of finding food, water and shelter for the original eighty pilgrims was formidable enough. But, though small, the procession was representative of much of India: there were Muslims; there were Sikhs; there was at least one Christian; most noteworthy of all, there were untouchables. To the high-caste Hindu pilgrims this last seemed startling, almost unacceptable. All their lives they had been taught to believe that they must shun contact with the untouchables; that they would be polluted, disgraced, if they consorted with them. Gandhi would have none of it. When the pilgrims stopped for the night in some wayside village he made a point of introducing the untouchables to the local dignitaries and making sure that they were as well treated as any of their companions. The procession left a mark behind it: in many villages functionaries who had been working with the British for many years resigned their posts in support of Gandhi, leaving an administrative vacuum that threatened the very basis of imperial society.

At sixty, Gandhi was the oldest of the marchers. He also turned out to be one of the fittest. The Viceroy was disappointed. "The will-power of the man must have been enormous to get him through his march," he told the Secretary of State for India. "I was always told that his blood pressure is dangerous and his heart none too good." Irwin had hoped that Gandhi would die *en route* or at least would have to retire to hospital: "It would be a very happy solution." Gandhi did not oblige; indeed, he seemed to gather strength as the march went on: the vision of this indomitable veteran striding forward day by day on his extraordinary mission caught the imagination not only of all India but of far beyond it. "I want world sympathy in this battle of Right against Might," he declared. By the time he reached the sea he had achieved his aim.

On the night of April 5, after twenty-four days, the procession reached the sea at Dandi. Over the last few days the numbers had been allowed to swell dramatically and there were several thousand enthusiastic followers when, at dawn the following morning, Gandhi walked onto the beach and picked up a small lump of salt. "Hail, Deliverer!" cried Mrs Sarojini Naidu as he did so. Jawaharlal Nehru, who was at Gandhi's side, was slightly less reverential. "We ultimately succeeded in producing some unwholesome stuff which we waved around in triumph and often auctioned for fancy prices . . . It was really immaterial whether the stuff was good or bad, the main thing was to commit a breach of the obnoxious Salt Laws." In fact what was left of the lump of salt was eventually sold at auction for 1,600 rupees, thus providing a useful reinforcement for the coffers of the liberation movement.

* * *

Of course the Salt March did not lead directly to the liberation of British India. It was to take more than fifteen years and a World War before independence was finally achieved. By that time Gandhi was an old man, though his energy and vitality would have done credit to somebody half his age. But more than any other single factor, even the Amritsar massacre, the march drew the attention of the world to the state of British India. Imperialism was still very much in the natural order of things at the beginning of the 1930s. To most Americans, it is true, the idea of empire seemed abhorrent, but it was not for them a pressing issue, they did not pay much attention to what was going on in the remoter reaches of the world. There were those in Britain, too, who believed that the Europeans had no right to impose their values on what Kipling disparagingly referred to as the "lesser breeds without the law". These were a small minority, however; to most Britons it seemed that their countrymen had not merely a right but a duty to bestow on the Indians the advantages of Western civilisation. The Salt March, with its discipline, its determination, its peaceful yet resolute defiance of British rule, for the first time led many Britons to question their countrymen's prerogative to ride roughshod over this vast and ancient civilisation. Gandhi in particular was invested by the march with something close to heroic status. It would be another seventeen years before Churchill's "seditious fakir" had been transformed into the man whom the last Viceroy, Louis Mountbatten, regarded with affection and something close to reverence, but the Salt March immeasurably enhanced his status in the eyes of the world. It did not fundamentally damage the foundations of British India, but it rocked them.

NOTES FOR FURTHER READING

Gandhi must rank with Napoleon and Jesus Christ when it comes to the number of books devoted to his doings. His own writings are, for the most part, hard going, though his autobiography, *The Story of My Experiments with Truth*, available in many editions and first published in 1930, is essential reading for any student of the period. Among the many biographies, Stanley Wolpert's *Gandhi's Passion* (Oxford 2001) is readable, reliable and relatively short. Judith Brown's *Gandhi. Prisoner of Hope* (Yale 1989) is sound if a little reverential; Michael Edwardes's *The Myth of the Mahatma* (London 1986), as its title suggests, is shorter on reverence (and in pages). Rajmohan Gandhi more recently contributed a massive biography of his grandfather (London 2007).

12

THE CHACO WAR

1932–5

On 14 June, 1932, a handful of Bolivian soldiers, wandering dispirit-edly around the Chaco desert, a largely deserted hinterland between Argentina, Bolivia and Paraguay, stumbled on a Paraguayan camp and chased its occupants from the scene. Nobody was killed or even injured, the territory was valueless, no issue of economic or material value was at stake. The war that followed lasted three years, bank-rupted both countries and cost some hundred thousand lives.

* * *

In hindsight it seems inevitable that at some point Bolivia and Paraguay would find themselves at war. Yet it was an adventure that neither country could afford. Bolivia was one of the poorest countries in the world. In theory its vast resources of tin should have guaranteed it prosperity, but the price of tin in the world markets plummeted and Bolivia's landlocked geography meant that the cost of getting its products onto the world markets was extravagantly high. Its population – a tiny three to four million: reliable and accurate statistics are hard to come by – was pre-dominantly Indian; the next largest, though far smaller, group was the *mestizos*, those of mixed Indian and Spanish blood;

A light machine-gun of the Bolivian army put to use as an anti-aircraft gun.

power was concentrated in the hands of an unhealthily small group of people of more or less unadulterated European stock. The Indians, by the will of their Spanish conquerors but also by their own volition, had remained largely unassimilated. "Sullen, suspicious and truculent," they were described by a historian from the United States, "their earthly possessions consist of a miserable hovel, a few sheep, llamas, pigs and hens, a small patch of potatoes and the ever-present pouch of coca leaves." Philip de Ronda, author of this unflattering description, was a committed supporter of Paraguay and thus unlikely to paint Bolivia in a favourable light, but it does seem that the Bolivian peasant was deprived not only of the amenities of civilised existence but of any serious prospect of bettering his condition.

By 1930 Bolivia had enjoyed something over a century of independence. "Enjoyed" is perhaps an ill-chosen word. Politically it was almost uniquely unstable: it had been ruled over by forty governments and had endured getting on for two hundred attempts to overthrow the – more or less – legitimate authorities. Daniel Salamanca, who became President in March 1931, was one of the more distinguished Bolivian leaders, but even he failed to maintain a commanding majority in the legislature and only the realisation that it would be unwise to attempt changing horses in the middle of an increasingly turbulent stream led to his continued hold on office.

Paraguay had a population far smaller even than that of its neighbour – something over a million – but the boundaries that marked the ethnic groups were less clearly marked. It too had suffered a series of short-lived governments interspersed with *coups d'état*, the latter tending to be bloodier and more embittered than their Bolivian counterparts. Bereft as it was of valuable mineral resources it depended almost entirely on agriculture for what little it enjoyed by way of prosperity. Its greatest natural asset was the River Paraguay, which joined the River Paraná, then the River Uruguay and finally reached the sea in the estuary of the River Plate. Paraguay, therefore, had access to the sea – a lengthy and expensive journey but still one giving it a considerable advantage over its less fortunate neighbour. At one time Bolivia had possessed a strip of the Pacific coast which included the port of Antofagasta, but a disastrous war with Chile had led to the loss of its western seabord and now the most realistic hope of securing access to the outside world seemed to be by way of the River Paraguay. Even if it managed to obtain a port on that river there would be another thousand miles or so to sail before the Atlantic was reached, but at least it would have established a secure route to the ocean. Bolivia's wish to enjoy that privilege is one of the underlying causes, some would say the most significant cause, of the Chaco War.

For the River Paraguay ran for some hundred and fifty miles along the eastern fringes of the ill-defined and supremely inhospitable region that gave its name to that war. The Chaco had very little else to commend it. It was vast: almost a hundred thousand square miles, nearly three times the size of Portugal. To the east, where it met the Andes, it had some tolerably cultivable grasslands; to the west, as it neared the river, there was also a belt of land where cattle could be allowed to roam, but by far the greater part of it was flat and near desert, without water for the most part of the year, then for the rainy season reduced to an impassable swamp. Unsurprisingly, it was sparsely populated, a few thousand nomadic Indians grazed their cattle on whatever vegetation they could discover. Two years before fighting began a Comintern report noted that "in the Chaco Boreal there is no population which can determine its own fate, as there is nothing but mosquitoes, crocodiles and oil". The report was perhaps a little too dismissive. Over the previous fifty years a trickle of settlers, mainly Paraguayan though with a handful of Bolivians as well, had been establishing themselves and their cattle on the empty plains. The Indian inhabitants – such few as there were – were in no position to assert their rights; the new arrivals made it clear that they expected the protection of their governments; a string of military outposts – *fortines* – was established, pushing further and further into the interior.

Neither country had an unequivocal claim to own the territory. In 1907 a rough-and-ready settlement had been arrived at which divided the Chaco into Paraguayan and Bolivian zones, but the treaty was never formally ratified and the advancing settlers, if they were even aware of the existence of a provisional frontier, did not allow it to deter them from taking possession of any territory that was, in practice if not legally, up for grabs. First blood was drawn early in 1927 when a Bolivian soldier shot and killed a young Paraguayan officer who had been captured and was trying to escape. The Bolivian government, by no means ready to go to war, apologised for the incident and released the other prisoners who had been taken in the same incident, but feelings ran high in both Asunción and La Paz and no effective steps were taken to demarcate a frontier or to prevent further skirmishes. Both sides overtly prepared for war, petty incidents continued to stoke the fires, at the end of 1928 a violent clash left fifteen Paraguayan dead and was followed by an air attack by Bolivian bombers on Bahía Negra, a port on the River Paraguay. The incident lacked drama, in that none of the bombs actually exploded, but it still marked a further step on the road to all-out war.

The other American countries were dismayed to discover that two of their members were thus at each other's throats. The Pan-American League, with the United States very much in the lead, brought pressure on both parties to reach a settlement. A Commission of Investigation and Reconciliation was set up in Washington: the Investigation element was relatively straight-forward; Reconciliation proved more difficult. A settlement was patched up but neither side believed that it was likely to last. Busily, Bolivia and Paraguay built up their armies in preparation for the inevitable war.

Bolivia had a head start. Trained on German lines and led by a German military mission, the Bolivian army had for some years been swollen by the rule – evaded without too much difficulty but still generally observed – that every young man should serve for two years as a soldier. The German element suggests efficiency and resolution – such attributes were not wholly lacking but the army was inadequately armed and almost entirely without artillery. What the Bolivians did have was an air force: only a score or so planes of which no more than a dozen were likely to be operational at any given moment, but including three large transport aircraft which played a vital role in moving men and materials around the vast areas of the Chaco. The Paraguayan army and air force were significantly smaller but better prepared for war: over the previous decade rearmament had been made the top priority at the expense of every other governmental activity. As important as anything were the two Paraguayan gunboats which had been bought from Italy and which ensured that their owner would have undisputed control over movements on the River Paraguay.

It was improbable that either army woud be strong enough entirely to defeat the other; it was certain that neither country could afford a war. Even if there had been significant advantages to be gained by victory it would have been economic madness for Paraguay and Bolivia to fight each other; as it was, fuelled by fear and mutual suspicion, the two countries committed themselves to a struggle that was bound to prove ruinous to victor and vanquished alike.

* * *

The petty skirmish described in the opening paragraph was the incident which turned increasing friction into open – if undeclared – war. The Bolivian authorities were reluctant to let this happen. When they heard that one of their regiments had stumbled on and evicted a handful of Paraguayans from their camp beside Lake Chuquisaca they instructed its commander, Major Moscoso, to withdraw and take up a defensive position well away from the Paraguayan troops. These orders, however, did not appeal to the firebrand Colonel Peñaranda, who was Major Moscoso's immediate superior. He played for time; pleaded that, if Moscoso withdrew, it would deprive the Bolivian troops of their main source of water, and in the meantime reinforced the advance guard and eagerly awaited a Paraguayan riposte.

Inevitably, it came. When the news reached Asunción that the Bolivians had attacked Paraguayan troops and occupied what was *de facto* if not *de jure* Paraguayan territory there was an explosion of popular indignation. Huge crowds of militant students and workers demanded that the insult be avenged. Even if Salamanca had been disposed to be cautious he would have found it difficult to restrain his indignant people; as it was, he was happy to go along with the national mood. "If a nation does not react in the face of attacks it does not deserve to be a nation," he ranted. "I invite you to swear that we will sacrifice all in the defence of the fatherland." He brushed aside the doubts of his military advisers, who knew only too well how ill-prepared the Paraguayan army was to go to war, declared a state of siege and dispatched two regiments – virtually all the trained troops that were available – to the front.

June, July and August were the dry season in the Chaco; from September onwards it would be increasingly difficult to transport troops or supplies by road, and war would consist of foot-slogging through what would become ever more of a swamp. If either side was to land a knockout blow it would have to be done quickly. Of the two, the Paraguayans seemed slightly more likely to bring it off. They enjoyed the advantage of shorter lines of supply and were able to concentrate their forces in the Chaco while the Bolivians were still recruiting and assembling an army which would be more numerous but less well-trained and well-equipped than its adversary. The first significant battle was for Boquerón, a miserable little Paraguayan village deep in the Chaco, which had been briefly occupied by Bolivian troops in 1928, abandoned with some relief after only a few weeks, then re-occupied at the end of July 1932. Its main asset from the point of view of its defenders was that it had a well which provided enough, if only just enough, water for the use of its garrison. The unfortunate besieging forces had to rely entirely on supply by road. Attempts by the Paraguayans to retake their village were pursued with vigour but singular ineptitude. First, their advancing troops were strafed by the Bolivian air force, an attack which cost the Paraguayans many lives and was even more damaging to the morale of their infantry who, till then, had barely seen a plane, let alone endured aerial attack. They managed still worse when they finally reached Boquerón, advancing blithely across what they thought was a deserted plain, only to discover that the Bolivians were well dug in and in a position to direct devastating fire at the advancing enemy. The total of Paraguayan casualties was relatively small, perhaps a hundred dead and three or four times as many wounded, but they had expected an easy victory and the blow to their pride was sharp indeed. It was only after a lengthy siege that the Bolivian garrison, running out of food and ammunition and with more than half its numbers dead or injured, gave up the struggle and surrendered.

In Asunción and La Paz the news of the fall of Boquerón was hailed or mourned as an event of earth-shaking consequence. In the neighbouring countries it was seen as something of considerable importance. In Europe it was almost entirely ignored. It is striking that events which so radically affected the lives of so many Bolivians and Paraguayans should have mattered so little to the outside world.

The Times of London, whose coverage of foreign affairs was at least as thorough as that of any other European newspaper, awarded the news of the fall of Boquerón four lines at the bottom of the page. The result of the municipal election in Sofia was given rather more extensive coverage; the antics of the Vicar of Stiffkey, who pranced naked in a barrel, received far more attention than either of these events. To the average Briton, if he knew of it at all, the war between Bolivia and Paraguay would have seemed a storm in a teacup, and a pretty inconsiderable teacup at that. If one was actually *in* the teacup things seemed very different. The homeland of neither country was overrun but the economic disruption and the cost in lives was almost intolerable. At first it seemed that the Paraguayans might bring off a rapid victory. Bolivian morale was low, discipline in its army was shaky, there was little appetite for war in the civilian population; the Paraguayans proved more ready to accept the realities of the barren wasteland in which they were fighting and adjust their tactics accordingly. They also possessed a weapon which the Bolivians initially lacked – the mortar. In the absence of anything remotely resembling heavy artillery, the mortar proved strikingly effective; demoralised and scarred, the Bolivians withdrew: casualties had been light on both sides, no territory of any consequence had changed hands, but the Paraguayans had drawn first blood.

Their victory proved to be far from decisive. For the next three years the war continued; first one side gaining an advantage, then the other, neither able to land anything that was approaching a knockout blow. Each side, from time to time, claimed to be on the verge of victory; in fact, both sides proved to be the losers. But there was another, perhaps more significant loser: the force that was supposed to regulate the international community. A war between two minor powers, both sides dependent on the outside world for the supply of arms, both with fragile economies susceptible to external pressure: it seemed a situation tailor-made for a decisive intervention by that amorphous yet potentially all-powerful entity that was emerging on the global scene – the League of Nations. The League had been founded at the beginning of 1920, a fruit of the Peace Conference that had ended the First World War. Its principal aim, as set out in its founding Covenant, was to prevent wars by collective security and disarmament and to provide a mechanism for the settling of international disputes by negotiation and arbitration. When Paraguay declared war on Bolivia in May 1933, Bolivia appealed to the League, asking that economic sanctions should be imposed on the country that had so clearly identified itself as the aggressor. The League, however, doubted whether the identification was as clear as all that. True, Paraguay had been the one formally to declare war, but a state of war had effectively existed long before that and the question of who had fired the first shot, let alone who was morally responsible, was far from settled. The League approached both parties and asked if they would agree to arbitration. Paraguay agreed, Bolivia did not refuse but hedged its acceptance with qualifications. In November 1933 a commission for the League arrived in Asunción on the first leg of a trip designed to impose a ceasefire and to establish a basis for arbitration. A precarious ceasefire was indeed achieved, the acceptance of arbitration proved more evasive.

In February 1934 the League put forward a draft peace treaty which would have involved both sides pulling back from confrontation. The armies were to be drastically reduced in size and the ultimate division of the disputed territory was to be referred to the International Court at The Hague. Neither Bolivia nor Paraguay overtly rejected the League's proposals; neither had any intention of accepting them in anything approaching their entirety. By March 1934 the League's Chaco Commission was in despair. Its members closed the office that they had established in Argentina and retreated to their respective capitals, leaving a skeleton staff to keep alive the possibility that serious talks might one day be resumed. Two months later the League called for an arms embargo to be applied to both participants. The United States, main supplier of weapons to both parties, enthusiastically supported the principle of the embargo; in practice, however, the flow of arms, though diminished, was far from halted. The League continued its efforts to impose a ceasefire. Inevitably, such a step seemed far more acceptable to the side that was temporarily in the weaker position. Bolivia accepted the proposal in principle; Paraguay rejected any compromise and, early in 1935, withdrew from the League of Nations. It was not until June of that year that it became obvious to everyone that an out-and-out victory would never be achieved by either side and that nothing was to be gained by continuing the sterile conflict.

* * *

Who won the Chaco War? "Nobody" is the short answer: it was inconceivable that anything would be gained by either party which could be remotely commensurate with the expense, loss of life and disruption of all economic activities that had occurred. Paraguay, which was left in control of most of the disputed territories, was slightly better placed to boast of victory: needless to say, it did so vociferously. Further vindication for its claims came when, after many months of fruitless bickering, the Bolivians finally abandoned their pretensions to establish their own port on the River Paraguay. In exchange, the Paraguayans promised that their former enemies would enjoy free access to the river, thus assuring the Bolivians of the practical, if not the juridical achievement of their ambitions. The peace, reported the leading La Paz daily newspaper, "has been received in Bolivia with a serene feeling of dignity that is far from conducive to displays of satisfaction and joy". There was rather more satisfaction and joy to be detected in Paraguay, but even there the prevailing feeling was one of intense relief that the war was over rather than jubilation that it had ended in victory.

Incredibly, it was not until 2009 that a treaty delimiting the boundaries between the two countries was signed and formally accepted in a ceremony in Buenos Aires. "This is a historic day for Bolivia and Paraguay," said the Bolivian President, Evo Morales, "a time of peace and friendship, of solidarity among peoples. The war between Paraguay and Bolivia was not triggered by the people but by the transnational corporations after our natural resources." It was convenient for both governments to place the blame for the war not on the Bolivian and Paraguayan leaders of the time but on the international oil companies. Nor were such claims wholly fantastical: Royal Dutch Shell and Standard Oil had indeed played a significant part in exacerbating the tension between the two countries. But they could only claim a small part of the credit: two peoples were suspicious of and ill-disposed towards each other; two weak governments were eager to accede to what they felt was the popular demand; two presidents saw themselves as potentially heroic figures whose reputations would be made for ever if they put themselves at the head of their nation and led it to victory. The Chaco War was unnecessary and largely futile but it was probably inevitable.

NOTES FOR FURTHER READING

Bruce W. Fareau's *The Chaco War* (London 1966) is the most balanced and comprehensive account of this little-studied war. Philip de Ronde's *Paraguay. A Gallant Little Nation* (New York 1935) is, as its title suggests, partisan in its presentation of the material but contains much of interest. A. de Quesada's *The Chaco War 1932–1935* (Oxford 2011) is little more than a pamphlet but provides the most up-to-date account of the conflict. John Sandor's *Bolivia's Radical Tradition* (University of Arizona Press 2009) concentrates on the Bolivian element and is thus a useful corrective to Philip de Ronde's Paraguayan paean.

13

HITLER TAKES POWER

1933

Shortly after noon on Monday, 30 January, 1933, a small group of middle-aged men filed into the office of the Reich President in Berlin. Field Marshal Paul von Hindenburg, the incumbent, greeted them with a short speech and, with a minimum of ceremony, sped them on their way again. "Hitler is Reich Chancellor. Just like a fairy tale!" recorded one of the visitors, Joseph Goebbels.

* * *

Fairy tale or nightmare, few would have predicted it even a year before, let alone have deemed it possible when Adolf Hitler was a child. His father had been a modestly successful civil servant, more than fifty years old when Adolf, the fourth child of a third marriage, was born on 20 April, 1889. Their home was on the border of Austria and Germany: Adolf was Austrian by birth but felt no particular allegiance to his natal country. His father seems to have been intellectually limited and something of a bully: Klara, his mother, did her best to provide the love that was so signally lacking in her husband but had been battered by an oppressive marriage into lacklustre acquiescence. It cannot have been a happy childhood and Adolf himself showed few signs that

Adolf Hitler gives a speech as work is begun on the Reichsautobahn Frankfurt–Heidelberg.

he was capable of transcending his experience and achieving any sort of distinction. His record at school was mediocre: he failed to gain the Leaving Certificate which was usually forthcoming for anyone of even the slightest ability and left school with no clear idea of how he was going to make his living. He wanted to be an artist, he declared; the flaw in this laudable ambition was that he had only meagre artistic talents. He failed to secure a place at the Academy of Fine Arts in Vienna, lived for a time in near destitution, then scraped a precarious livelihood by producing and – sometimes – selling tawdry reproductions of the paintings in Vienna's many galleries and museums. By the time he moved to Munich in 1913 he had achieved little or nothing and seemed destined to spend his life as an impecunious hack, scraping a living from work which would have seemed ignoble to any artist of even modest talents or ambitions.

It was the war that saved him. He took it for granted that the German cause must be the cause of justice and reason but showed little interest in the issues that had made war inevitable. War, to his mind, was welcome, not because it was a just war or a necessary war, but because it *was* war, because it provided a fire in which the sins of a decadent people could be purged and in which the grandeur of the nation would be recaptured. War was necessary if Germany was to fulfil the destiny which it had arrogated to itself since it had united under the leadership of Prussia, and take on the leadership of Europe, the leadership of the world. War was necessary – though he probably never saw it in such stark terms himself – if Adolf Hitler was to escape from the trammels of *petit bourgeois* respectability and achieve greatness. "I am not ashamed to acknowledge," he wrote in his autobiography and political testament, *Mein Kampf*, "that I was carried away by the enthusiasm of the moment and that I sank down upon my knees and thanked heaven for the favour of having been permitted to live in such a time."

Not that his wartime experiences brought him anything approaching grandeur. He had nothing to be ashamed of in his years as a soldier. He had been one of the first to volunteer for military service – in the German rather than the Austrian army – and within a few weeks of his joining up was promoted to corporal. That was the end of it, however. Perhaps he refused further promotion because he was reluctant to leave his regiment; perhaps it was felt that he lacked the qualities that would have justified his going any further. At any rate it was as a corporal that he saw out the rest of the war. But nobody ever questioned his courage or his ability to perform his duties; he was awarded an Iron Cross Second Class (the best that was available given his lowly rank) and was one of the last to admit that defeat had become inevitable. While the war lasted he was inflexible in his commitment to the struggle and was outraged when, at Christmas 1914, German and British troops abandoned their trenches and fraternised freely in no-man's-land. "There should be no question of something like that during the war," he expostulated. When finally the war ended he was prominent among those who refused to accept that the German army had been defeated but instead clung to the conviction that it had been betrayed by ignoble politicians. Most Germans in 1918 felt that they had had enough war to last them for a lifetime; Hitler never doubted that there must be another round and that next time Germany would be triumphant.

November 1918 found him in hospital suffering, according to *Mein Kampf*, at least, from injuries caused by mustard gas. He had no future as a soldier – the German army had more or less ceased to exist; he had very little money; he had only the most exiguous qualifications for any serious profession. The prospects could hardly have been bleaker. Within three years he had become one of the most prominent of German politicians; within twelve he was on the brink of absolute power.

* * *

If there is one thing, more than any other, that can be held responsible for this striking metamorphosis, it is that Hitler discovered that he could speak. "Speak" for him meant to hold forth on a platform. He was not a master of lucid argument – in a small discussion group he was rarely among the more impressive performers and could sometimes be notably inept – but confront him with a mass audience, even an audience that was initially hostile, and he was at once transformed. Even the most sophisticated could find themselves overwhelmed by the demagogic passion of his delivery but it was on the middle-classes, above all the lower middle-classes, that his impact was strongest. Karl Mayr was Hitler's immediate superior in the intelligence division of Germany's ministry of defence, the *Reichswehr*. Hitler, he noted in 1920, "has become a motive force, a popular speaker of the first rank". It seems to have been Mayr who was the first to see Hitler's potential and selected him as one of an elite squad charged with brain-washing those who had been tainted by Bolshevik propaganda. Hitler took to the task with relish and swiftly learned to associate, almost to identify, the Bolsheviks with what he perceived as another, more insidious but no less threatening sector of society, the Jews.

Hitler's anti-Semitism had grown upon him before he left Vienna to go to Munich. In *Mein Kampf* he describes how one day he "encountered a phenomenon in a long kaftan and wearing black sidelocks . . . I watched the man stealthily and cautiously, but the longer I gazed at this strange countenance and examined it section by section, the more the question shaped itself in my brain: is this a German?" Unsurprisingly, his conclusion was that this was not a German; on the contrary, it was something that he saw to be inimical to all that was best in German culture and society, it was a Jew. Once this revelation had dawned on him he quickly perceived the terrifying scale of the threat. The fatherland was in peril: the Jews would stop at nothing to contaminate the purity of its blood and to destroy its most cherished traditions. The Jews, wrote Hitler, "were responsible for bringing negroes into the Rhineland with the ultimate idea of bastardising the white race, which they hate, and thus lowering its cultural and political level so that the Jew might dominate." They had insinuated themselves into positions of power within the worlds of finance and politics and had acquired a dangerous influence in the popular press that was burgeoning and beginning to shape the views of the proletariat. They must be stopped; ultimately Germany must be purged of their unholy presence.

Hitler was not the only man to have perceived this threat. Anti-Semitism was already rife in Vienna, where there was a large Jewish population – "the giant city seemed the embodiment of racial desecration," wrote Hitler. There were other demagogues, in particular one of Hitler's earliest idols, Karl Lueger, who disliked the Jews and rejoiced in the opportunities which the Jewish community – rich, prominent and economically powerful out of all proportion to its numbers – gave for whipping up the hostile passions of the mob. But with Hitler it became an obsession. He equated Semitism with Marxism – a position that might seem difficult to maintain given the traditional enthusiasm of one party for the accumulation of capital and the other for taking it away again, but one which he maintained with unquestioning conviction. As with the other Nazis, his political philosophy was predominantly negative – he placed the emphasis almost entirely on denouncing those elements which he felt were destructive to German society and paid little attention to the steps that would have to be taken if Germany was to achieve prosperity and stability.

Such an attitude was not likely to achieve much success while the country itself remained prosperous and stable – why waste energy on combating the Jews and Marxists if Germany was patently doing well in spite of their malign activities? Everything changed, however, when things began to go badly. If the national economy was in trouble it was only too likely that the underprivileged would seek to identify scapegoats on whom they could blame their misfortunes. Hitler's fortunes waxed and waned in inverse proportion to the success of the German economy.

In 1923 it seemed that things could hardly have been worse for Germany or better for Hitler. At the end of the war the rate of exchange had been four marks to the dollar; in 1921 and 1922 inflation gathered speed at a rate which was at first alarming, then terrifying and finally catastrophic. By early 1923 the dollar was worth more than seven thousand marks. The French occupation of the industrial district of the Ruhr as punishment for German failure to keep up with its reparation payments compounded the disaster; by November 1923 the mark was virtually worthless, a hundred and thirty thousand million to the dollar. The savings of all but the most plutocratic Germans with access to foreign exchange were wiped out, normal financial transactions became impossible, barter took the place of conventional sales and purchases, millions of Germans were close to starvation. The government appeared to be incapable of providing even those minimum conditions which were essential for civilised existence. In such circumstances, anyone who offered convincingly to fill the gap would surely be acceptable?

In fact, in spite of the dire plight of the economy, it transpired that the time was not yet right for the overthrow of the government. Hitler overplayed his hand. He failed to appreciate the steadfastness of the army when it came to supporting the legitimate authorities, he overestimated the cohesion of his followers and the attraction of the Nazi movement to the proletariat. He struck too early. The attempted Munich Beer Hall putsch that November failed; he found himself in the dock, accused of high treason; he was sentenced to five years' imprisonment. But though his timing had been wrong, disaster was soon turned to triumph. The goverment seemed to be consumed by the conviction of its own impotence. It shrank from decisive action. Though Hitler was found guilty he had been allowed to dominate the court; it was he who had won the approval of much of the public and had emerged the hero. Though sentenced to five years, he only served nine months; while in prison he was allowed to conduct himself not as a convict but as a party leader in temporary exile. The time that he did not spend writing *Mein Kampf* was devoted to political activities. In his absence the Party languished – he would not have had it otherwise, since a Nazi Party that could flourish without Hitler at its head would have been, in his eyes at least, a Party lacking its soul – but it remained intact, ready to be recalled to full life when its leader was once more at the helm. "The moment he is set free," read a Bavarian police report, "Hitler will . . . again become the driving force of new and serious public riots and a menace to the security of the state."

A menace he certainly was, but by the middle of 1924 inflation had been checked. Hitler emerged from prison into a Germany less vulnerable to violent upset than had been the case a year or two before. A new and more lenient reparations agreement had been negotiated, the Ruhr had been evacuated, in September 1926 Germany took its place as a member of the League of Nations. The President elected in April 1925, the veteran Field Marshal von Hindenburg, had been backed rather unenthusiastically by the Nazis but soon showed himself disappointingly inclined to support the democratic constitution and distance himself from his more *outré* right-wing supporters. Liberal Germany congratulated itself that the Nazi menace had been eliminated before it had really been given a chance to establish itself. The swastikas and storm troops had disappeared, wrote the novelist Stefan Zweig, and the name of Adolf Hitler had fallen almost into oblivion. "Nobody thought of him any longer as a possible in terms of power."

Even when Zweig wrote he was overstating his case. At no

point had Hitler fallen into oblivion or anything close to it. Though his country might have seemed less immediately vulnerable to Nazi blandishments, he himself had been fortified by his ordeal. He emerged from prison with confidence in his destiny reinforced. Only when it came to the ways by which he planned to achieve his ends had Hitler's thinking changed. The army, he concluded, must be central to his ambitions; never again would he seek to grasp power unless assured of its support or, at least, benevolent neutrality. Even more important, power was to be gained by constitutional means. Once this had been achieved, then such old-fashioned methods could safely be abandoned, but until the Nazis secured power any direct contravention of the law must be avoided. For several years after his release from prison Hitler took things slowly. His new tactics worked. Though there were only a dozen or so National Socialist deputies in the Reichstag in the late 1920s, in the country the Nazi Party was growing, gradually at first, then, as Germany slipped back into inflation, more and more rapidly. By the end of 1930 it boasted more than a million members.

But Zweig was not wholly out of touch with reality. As late as 1927 the Minister of the Interior described the National Socialist Party as "numerically insignificant", a "radical-revolutionary splinter group incapable of exerting any noticeable influence on the great mass of the population". In the May 1928 elections the Nazis polled well under a million votes and were one of the smallest parties represented in the Reichstag. Hitler himself, though to some extent he had succeeded in establishing himself as a national figure, was still one of the lesser political leaders, not considered by many of his contemporaries as somebody who needed to be taken very seriously. Hitler, said the liberal newspaper *Frankfurter Zeitung*, was "a dangerous fool". One might argue that he was mad but hardly that he was a fool; that he was dangerous was becoming more obvious by the day.

His advance towards power can be measured against the decline of Field Marshal Paul von Hindenburg. Hindenburg was once a titanic figure. In the last years of the First World War he and General Ludendorff had enjoyed something close to absolute power. Ludendorff had experienced electoral disaster in 1925 and was no longer a force to be reckoned with; in the same year and at the age of seventy-eight Hindenburg had found himself elected President. It was not an office that he had sought and he accepted it only out of a sense of duty to his country. He would have done better to refuse it. He was old and tired, old even beyond his years. Never the most astute of political manoeuv-rers, he now did little more than provide cover under which Hitler could accumulate power. He consistently underes-timated Hitler, dismissing him loftily as the "Bavarian corporal" and seeking to deny him any important office, but his own candi-date for the office of Chancellor, Franz von Papen, was a second-rate politician who was unable to offer any serious opposition to Hitler's ambitions. Probably there was no German prominent in public life who could have checked Hitler in his final ascent to power; certainly Hindenburg was not the man to do it.

Once again it was the economic situation that opened the path for Hitler. The downturn that followed the Wall Street Crash of 1929 had not been a purely American phenomenon. Throughout 1931 and 1932 conditions grew worse by the day. By the end of 1931 there were more than five million registered unemployed and many of those in work were under-employed or felt their jobs to be in jeopardy. At the election at the end of July, 1931, the Nazis had gained ground significantly, more than doubling the number of their seats in the Bundestag. Papen hoped that he could remain in office, taking the Nazis into his government but retaining control of the most important ministries. Hitler would have none of it; he sensed that his time had come and he was not going to be satisfied by anything less than absolute power. Kurt von Schleicher, the general who saw himself as the political voice of the Army and the real power behind Hindenburg, deluded himself that he could manage Hitler and enlist the Nazi Party in a grand coalition that would restore stability to the country. Schleicher, reported the French military attaché, believed that Hitler "knows very well how to distinguish between the demagoguery suitable to a young Party and the needs of national and international life". The Nazi leader's bark, Schleicher maintained, was worse than his bite. Like the young lady from Riga who went for a walk with a tiger, it turned out that Schleicher had misjudged both the strength of his own position and the unscrupulousness of the other party: when the walk was over the smile was on the face of the tiger.

The breakthrough came in 1932. Schleicher accepted the need to conciliate the Nazis but still hoped that they could be persuaded to moderate their policies, to play by the rules. If Hitler would support Hindenburg for another two years, until lasting economic stability had been restored, then the way would be open for the Nazis to take part in the government of the country, perhaps even to take power. To Schleicher this seemed a generous offer, but it was not good enough for the Nazis. Hitler indicated that he was ready to let Hindenburg remain as President but only if the present administration was dismissed and new elections held. In fact two elections followed, neither giving a convincing majority to any party; but when the polls closed after the second election the Nazis had secured nearly 13.5 million votes. They were not yet strong enough to govern Germany single-handed but they *were* strong enough to make the government of Germany impossible without their co-operation. "We have a difficult decision to make," wrote the future propaganda chief, Joseph Goebbels: "Coalition with the Centre and power or opposition to the Centre without power." They chose the first, but "coalition" was a word that could be interpreted in many ways. The Nazis had no intention of sharing effective power with anyone. Temporary alliances might be tolerated but they intended that any such ally should either be subsumed within the Party or ruthlessly discarded as soon as it seemed expedient. It was a risky policy, but Hitler believed that the risk was well worth taking. There was a feeling of urgency within the Party; a belief that an opportunity existed that, if it were missed, might never recur. "We must come to power in the foreseeable future," concluded Goebbels. "Otherwise we'll win ourselves to death in elections."

Hitler hardly took any trouble to conceal from Papen that he saw the latter's tenure of office as Chancellor as being limited. The two men had not even met before Papen took office. When they did have their first discussions Papen was surprised by what he saw as Hitler's "ordinariness". "I could detect no inner quality which might explain his extraordinary hold on the masses," he remembered. "Although I had heard much about the magnetic quality of his eyes, I do not remember being impressed by them."

But he recognised that, whatever Hitler's limitations, it would be impossible to rule without Nazi support and he did not delude himself into thinking that that support would continue once Hitler had concluded that the time had come to take the reins of power himself.

Yet another election marked a further step forward for the Nazis. At the end of July 1932 they once more increased their vote to some 14 million, nearly twice as large a share of the electorate as could be boasted by their nearest rivals, the Social Democrats. The other parties comforted themselves with the reflection that Hitler had still not achieved an overall majority and was never likely to do so. His success had peaked, concluded the British Ambassador. He "seems now to have exhausted his reserves. He has swallowed up the small bourgeois parties of the Middle and the Right, and there is no indication that he will be able to effect a breach in the Centre, Communist and Socialist parties." For a few months it seemed as if the Ambassador might be right. Germany, in the summer and autumn of 1932, was racked by disorder, a transport strike paralysed much of the country, the Nazis found themselves linked with the Communists in the popular mind as being disorderly elements which sought to impede rather than strengthen the forces of legitimate government. When the fifth election was held, in November, the Nazis lost votes, still remaining by far the largest party but with their lead over the Nationalists and, more significantly, the Communists notably reduced.

It was probably the growing strength of the Communists that saved Hitler's bacon. Papen, he argued, by his reactionary policies was driving the electorate towards the extreme left;

only an independent Party, unfettered by the shibboleths of the traditional right, could hope to check the resurgent forces of Marxism. The argument made sense to the floating voter, who viewed with dismay the drift towards the left; more significantly, it made sense to many of Papen's followers, who feared that he personally might be becoming the principal obstacle in the way of establishing a stable government. Papen tried out the possibility of a halfway house, offering Hitler and one or two of his followers important posts in a coalition government. Hitler would have none of it; the time, he felt, was ripe for the Nazis to take power; he would not merely stay out of but would relentlessly oppose any government that did not have him at its head. In the end Papen gave way, assuring himself as he did so that it would quickly be shown that the Nazis were unable to govern the country effectively and that, in the not so distant future, he would be returned to power. Little though he liked it, Hindenburg could hardly reject such advice from his incumbent Chancellor.

There was still some haggling to be done and other permutations were considered and rejected. Schleicher had not lost confidence in himself as a power broker and at one point aimed higher and served briefly as Chancellor himself. It could not last, however. On 4 January, 1933, Hitler and Papen met secretly in Cologne. Papen tried out the possibility that he and Hitler should serve as joint Chancellors; a proposition which was swiftly rejected and which he can hardly have imagined would be accepted. Still he clung on to the hope that he could continue in office and that Hitler might somehow be persuaded for a time at least to play the part of benevolent neutral. It took another two or three weeks for this last hope to die, but by the time that Hitler met secretly with Oskar von Hindenburg, the President's son, on January 22, Papen had privately accepted that Hitler must become Chancellor and that the most he could hope for was a place for himself and his closest allies in the new government. A few days later he told Hitler's chief negotiator, Joachim von Ribbentrop, that this was now his view. "The recognition by Papen is, I believe, the turning point," wrote Ribbentrop exultantly.

Hitler was surprisingly reasonable when it came to discussing who would fill what posts in the new Cabinet and Papen took fresh comfort from what he saw as evidence of Nazi moderation. "You are playing into Hitler's hands," one of Papen's colleagues told him. "You are mistaken," Papen replied. "We've hired him." Hitler was well content that Papen should continue in this comforting delusion. At eleven o'clock in the morning of Monday, 30 January, he and the members of his future Cabinet filed into the chambers of the Reich President. Hitler made a brief statement promising to uphold the constitution and to govern in the interests of the nation as a whole and not of the Nazi or any other party. Hindenburg nodded with an approval that must have been tinged with scepticism. "And now, gentlemen, forward with God," he exhorted his new Cabinet.

* * *

It is important that those who see Hitler as a brutal dictator, indifferent to the true needs and wishes of his people, should remember that he was constitutionally elected. Admittedly, he won office having gained only 37 per cent of the votes, but this was considerably more than any other German politician had achieved. It was Hitler who insisted from the moment he took power that his government should be validated by a further election. Once the Nazis were established in power, however, any pretence of deference to constitutional values or liberal ideas was swiftly jettisoned. "From now on," Hitler proclaimed, "we shall wage a relentless war of purification against the forces that remain bent on undermining our culture." Pre-eminent among such forces were, of course, the Communists and the Jews, and these became his prime targets in the battle that he now waged to eliminate anything which did not fit in with his vision of a refulgent Aryan paradise. The leaders of the other European powers watched aghast as the full horrors of Fascism were revealed. They told themselves hopefully that the fires would soon burn out and that, even if they did not, their evil would be confined to Germany. Even then, however, there were a few who saw that Fascism could not peacefully co-exist for long with its democratic neighbours. It took only a few years for them to be proved right. From the moment that Hitler took office as Chancellor it was a question of when, not whether, the Second World War would start.

NOTES FOR FURTHER READING

The birth pangs of Fascist Germany are recorded in innumerable histories and it is hard to know what to recommend. So far as biographies of Hitler are concerned, among the best established are Alan Bullock's *Hitler, A Study in Tyranny* (London 1952); Joachim Fest's *Hitler* (London 1973) and Ian Kershaw's *Hitler 1889–1936* (London 1999). Richard Evans's *The Coming of the Third Reich* (London 2003) provides a comprehensive survey of the subject while J. M. Roberts's *A History of Europe* (Oxford 1996) offers a masterly background to this, as to several other chapters.

14

THE LONG MARCH

1934

Late in the afternoon of Tuesday, 16 October, 1934, a Chinese Communist soldier stepped tentatively onto the pontoon bridge that had been hurriedly rigged up at Yudu across the River Mei Jiang. He was embarking on an epic trek that was to take him six thousand miles towards the north, almost to the frontier with Soviet Russia. The Long March had begun.

* * *

Who was the enemy and from whom was he escaping? The answer to both questions should have been the Japanese. Throughout 1931 the Japanese had been infiltrating Manchuria, the vast and sparsely populated province in the north-east of China which had largely been controlled by the Russians since 1900 but which was the homeland of the Manchu dynasty and therefore, in the eyes of Peking at least, quintessentially Chinese. In September infiltration gave way to out-and-out invasion, and within a few weeks Japanese control of the province was complete. Such overt aggression should have united the Chinese in defence of their beloved fatherland, but the Communist leader, Mao Zedong, had other, more immediate adversaries whom he

Soldiers crossing a mountain in Western China in 1935.

feared still more greatly than the alien Japanese. China was a country riven by civil war and it was the enemy within that most immediately preoccupied Mao.

Twenty, even ten years before, there would have been no reason to suppose that it would be Mao who would be playing so prominent a role. His origins were undistinguished and his abilities, though from the start obviously considerable, did not seem to mark him out as a leader of men. Though Mao liked to pretend that he had risen from the humblest level of society, his father had in fact been a prosperous farmer. Not much love was lost between father and son, but Mao's father at least ensured that his son had an excellent education. Mao did not immediately shine, however. It was not until he was in his early twenties that he gave his contemporaries reason to believe that he might be anything very far out of the ordinary. He started his professional life as a teacher and soon fell under the influence of Professor Chan, a Marxist intellectual who, as much as any other individual, was responsible for the growth of China's Communist Party, the C.C.P. Mao himself was not a founder member of the Party but he joined very near the beginning and, by the age of twenty-seven, was established as a figure of some stature and one of its more successful propagandists.

He was not the only young man to be making a name for himself in Chinese politics. Chiang Kai-shek had been born in 1887, some six years before Mao, into a family that was better off and slightly grander but was still part of what, in Europe, might have been described as the *haute bourgeoisie*. There, however, any similarity ended. Chiang became a professional soldier, rose swiftly and was put in charge of a mission to Soviet Russia. He disliked the experience intensely and returned a passionate anti-Communist. Soon he became a member of the right-wing Nationalist party, the Kuomintang, usually referred to as the K.M.T. Though both men firmly espoused their respective causes, neither was by nature a dogmatist. When Mao's Russian backers insisted that, in the short term at any rate, the Chinese Communists should work with rather than against the K.M.T., he was, seemingly at least, happy to accept the ruling. It was not until April 1927, when Chiang broke with his Communist allies and began a ferocious purge of Party members, that Mao and Chiang emerged as enemies, leaders of the two parties that were to dispute the future of China. Their competition, all-important as it seemed in Peking, did not mean much to the bulk of the Chinese population, some 480 million strong in 1927, who cared little whether the Communists or the Nationalists ran their country. The vast majority asked only to be left in peace. Modest though this wish might seem, however, there was little chance that it would be granted. Huge though China was, it was not big enough to hold both Chiang and Mao; until one or other had asserted his authority, until a Communist or a Nationalist government had been established, the country would be perpetually riven by civil war.

It was Chiang who at first made the running. The Nationalists were better organised, more numerous and in control of most of China's armed forces. They were ruthless in their resolve to eliminate Communism for once and for all and, for the purposes of their operations, the term "Communist" was applied to almost anyone who did not subscribe wholeheartedly to their precepts. In Shanghai, the heartland of Chinese Communism,

Chiang first worked with the Communists until he had secured a grip on the city, then turned on them and massacred several hundred of their leaders. For those who dwell on the peculiar nastiness of the Chinese Communist regime it is salutary to remember that, atrocity for atrocity, the Nationalists were little, if at all behind.

Nor were the Japanese invaders any more genteel in their practices. By the end of 1931 it was becoming clear that they were not going to confine themelves to operations in Manchuria; in early 1933 they were already forcing their way across the Great Wall into China proper. Still, the Chinese remained preoccupied by their internal differences; the only major battle of 1934 was between Communists and Nationalists. It ended in a decisive victory for the Nationalists. Mao concluded that, as things stood, he could never hope to achieve victory in outright battle. His objective must be to disengage and then to extricate as much of his army as he could to the North, where, eventually, he could hope to secure some support from the Soviet Union. Even as the crow flies that would have involved a journey of eight or nine hundred miles, but Mao was not to be afforded the luxury of taking the shortest route. Whichever way he wished to go, it seemed that an obdurate and numerically more powerful enemy awaited him. At first he seems to have believed that he could force his way through by the most direct route, but though he each time managed to make some headway the cost in lives was formidably high and the lack of a loyal heartland meant that he could not recruit new troops with the ease enjoyed by the Nationalist armies. He started his march some 100,000 strong, a figure that included many camp followers, who would be of little or no use in battle; within a few weeks he had lost 30,000 men and most of his artillery. But still the Communist army survived, its morale surprisingly high. It seems that the Nationalists shrank from engaging in an all-out battle that might, though at great cost to themselves, have destroyed the enemy.

The March was not conducted along well-paved roads with all the appurtenances of civilisation conveniently to hand; it straggled along mountainous paths and desert tracks, sometimes following nothing but what seemed to be the line of least resistance. It was every man for himself; anyone who could not keep up fell by the wayside, to be imprisoned or, more often, murdered by the Nationalist troops or to depend on the uncertain benevolence of the local villagers. It was every woman for herself, too; the March included several thousand wives or would-be wives who kept up only with the greatest difficulty, knowing that if they fell into the hands of the enemy then rape was the best that they could hope for. One woman who suffered as much as any was Mao's then wife. She had set out with the rest but was pregnant and found it difficult to keep up. Mao made some provision for her welfare, but when she eventually gave birth and then had to leave her baby with a local family he seems to have made no attempt to comfort her. To be fair, he had other things on his mind, but even at the best of times he was not the sort of man who would devote much of his time and energy to the succouring of those who suffered in his cause. He Zizhen remained with the March and was later severely injured by shrapnel from a bomb dropped by a Nationalist aircraft. The doctors recommended that she should be left behind; Mao disliked the idea that his wife might fall into the hands of Chiang's men and ordered that she should be carried along with the March in a litter. To everyone's surprise, and possibly her own regret, she survived, to exist precariously on the fringes of Mao's life for many years to come. For some of the time at least Mao himself enjoyed the luxury of being carried in a litter but he was generally perceived as sharing the dangers and discomfort of the rank and file. Certainly his popularity remained high: for most of the Communist soldiers Mao was the heroic leader who could do no wrong and whose setbacks were due only to the overwhelming strength of the enemy.

By this time – in late April 1935 – the Communist leadership was in disarray. Most of the commanders were convinced that the best, indeed the only rational, course was to continue to push northwards into Sichuan; Mao, almost alone, insisted that the proper policy was to retreat southwards towards Vietnam. It was a testimony to Mao's powers of leadership, if not his skills as a strategist, that for a long time his view prevailed. In the end, though, the united determination of his colleagues wore down his opposition. Their arguments were fortified by the tactics of the Nationalists, who seemed more bent on shepherding the Communists northwards than on engaging them in a major battle that might have destroyed the enemy but only at enormous cost to themselves. The Communists survived. There was much bitter fighting and the core of their army was reduced to a mere 30,000 men, but to the end it remained a cohesive and battle-hardened unit.

Perhaps from the point of view of China, the most significant feature of the Long March was that it confirmed Mao as the ultimate leader of the Party and the nation. At the outset he had been at most *primus inter pares*; hardly, indeed, even that. Zhou

En-lai was still effectively in charge of the army, Mao was little more than political commissar. Apart from Zhou, there were several other generals who felt themselves to be at least as well if not better qualified than Mao to assume supreme command. Even his present position did not seem particularly secure. He had been excluded from the Politburo and at one point put briefly under house arrest. His preferred policy of seemingly endless retreat, luring the enemy deeper and deeper into territory which they could never hope fully to control, had largely been abandoned. He was, if not in disgrace, then certainly regarded as a man who had had his chance and had blown it. He was a sick man, too; barely recovered from a severe bout of malaria, dependent on those who carried his litter if he was to retain his position among the marchers. Yet somehow, as all seemed to be in disarray around him, he managed to retain his vision and gradually to impose himself upon the heterogeneous bunch of mavericks and desperadoes who made up the larger part of the Commmunist leadership. It was thanks to Mao more than to any other individual that China stayed in the fight.

* * *

His prospects, and the prospects for the Communist cause as a whole, still looked bleak. Mao's army, the Central Red Army, was in grave disarray, reduced in numbers to something under ten thousand, its members deprived of almost everything except the arms that they could carry and sometimes without even those. The other substantial Communist force, the Fourth Front army under Zhang Guotao, had initially survived rather better but it suffered severely in the course of 1936 and by the time that all the Communist armies joined together they numbered little more than thirty thousand. But they were still an effective force; their morale was strikingly high; they were, if not united, then at least prepared to agree that their common enemy, the Japanese, must be the first to be combated and that internal dissension between the Chinese factions could be left to be sorted out until after the country had been liberated from the invader.

Even by the end of 1936 that seemed a remote prospect, and things got rapidly worse. The Japanese appeared unbeatable. In July 1937 they marched into Peking, in the course of the next year they occupied many of the principal cities. China, in short, had lost the war – except that China could never lose the war, was too huge a country to admit the possibility that it could ever finally be subjugated by another power. But nor could it ever hope, single-handed, to win the war. It took Japan's involvement in another, still greater conflict and the cataclysmic horror of the nuclear bomb, finally to destroy its power and to bring about its departure from the Chinese mainland. It was not until late in 1949 that the Nationalists were chased ignominiously to their last redoubt in Formosa and Mao was able to proclaim to the world that the People's Republic of China was entering the ranks of the superpowers. But from the moment that the first steps had been taken on the Long March, some fifteen years earlier, Mao had never doubted that, in the long run, it would prove to be a march to victory.

NOTES FOR FURTHER READING

The most comprehensive, if also the most hostile, biography of Mao Zedong is that by Jung Chang and Jon Halliday, *Mao. The Unknown Story* (London 2005). Dennis Bloodworth's *The Messiah and the Mandarins* (London 1982) appeared more than thirty years ago but is still well worth reading. *The Cambridge History of China,* Volume 13, Part 2, ed. John K. Fairbank and Albert Feuerwerker (Cambridge 1986) provides an excellent study of China between 1912 and 1949.

15

ITALY INVADES ABYSSINIA

1935

Early in the morning of 3 October, 1935 General Emilio De Bono, commander of the Italian army in its East African colony of Eritrea, ordered his troops to advance into the neighbouring country of Abyssinia. He was confronted by an army that was numerically much larger but from every other point of view was pitifully ill equipped to repel the invasion of a major European power. In military terms, the action was of trivial import; its importance lay in its revelation of Mussolini's swelling ambitions and the significance that these were to hold for Europe and, eventually, the world.

* * *

In a continent which, for more than a century, had been the victim of rapacious invaders from the north, Abyssinia was almost unique in having preserved its independence. Its ruling dynasty, the Habesha, had been in power for some seven hundred years and claimed descent from King Solomon. Not even the most patriotic Abyssinian would have maintained, or have wished to maintain, that his country was run on what a European might have considered "modern lines", but it was unequivocally a viable and independent state. In 1923 it had

Abyssinians saluting a giant picture of Benito Mussolini, (wearing his most determined expression) in the newly conquered territory in Northern Abyssinia.

joined the League of Nations: ironically enough, in view of the fact that members of the League were specifically precluded from going to war with each other, Italy had been to the fore in promoting Abyssinian entry. To gild this lily, five years later the two countries had signed a treaty, committing themselves to twenty years of friendship.

In November 1930 the Emperor Haile Selassie, King of Kings, Lion of Judah, had been crowned in Addis Ababa. Dignitaries from the world over had flocked to attend the ceremony: Italy was represented by its King's cousin, the Prince of Udine; Great Britain by another royal prince, the Duke of Gloucester. Such attendance did not necessarily imply any strong approval of the regime – Abyssinia, wrote a correspondent to *The Times*, "is a byword for disorder and barbarity: the disorder of feudal and tribal anarchy and the barbarity of the slave trade" – but it did demonstrate unequivocally that, in the eyes of the world, in the eyes of Italy, the country was there to stay.

In spite of the fact that it was led by a royal prince, the Italian delegation at the Coronation must have been ill at ease. Italy had a long-standing grudge to settle. Some forty years earlier an Italian army had advanced from its colony of Eritrea into Tigre, one of the two kingdoms of which Abyssinia at that time consisted. At first all went smoothly; what little opposition the invading force encountered was easily brushed aside. General Baratieri, the Italian commander, hungry for glory and urged on by a triumphantly expansionist government in Rome, pushed on with the blithe assurance that no native force could possibly present a serious challenge. Then the tide began to turn and, at Adowa, he found himself confronted by an Abyssinian army four or five times as large a his own. Defiantly he attacked and was over-whelmingly defeated: six thousand Italian soldiers died, the rest fled back to Eritrea. An uneasy peace was patched up and lasted until 1935, but Mussolini resented the fact that, while Britain, France and Belgium had built up large and profitable African empires, Italy could only boast of a relatively minor colony to the east of the continent. If that holding was to be expanded, it could only be at the expense of Abyssinia.

In spite of this, a larger Italian empire was not Mussolini's first preoccupation. "It is necessary," he had pronounced, "that the turbulent and megalomaniac Serbs be reduced to their pro-portions!" To achieve this end, he sought to build up an Italian area of influence in Eastern Europe which would make him the effective ruler of Greece, Yugoslavia and Turkey. Unfortunately for him his putative partners in this ambitious enterprise showed little eagerness to rally under the Italian banner, Yugoslavia proving particularly contumacious. Mussolini did not doubt that a war in the Balkans would eventually be necessary but, in the meantime, he felt that an African campaign would provide some easy glory and be good practice for the more serious business that lay ahead. It was, he told the Senate in May 1935, "precisely in order to be confident in Europe that we intend to secure our back in Africa". The reasoning was obscure – it is hard to see who posed a threat to his "back in Africa", if indeed he could be said to have had a back in Africa at all – but the implication that an African campaign would be a useful if not essential prelim-inary to a war in Europe was plain to see.

During the second half of 1934 and in 1935 Italy had built up its forces in Eritrea. Mussolini claimed that his intentions were purely defensive: the Abyssinian army was ever more threatening, incursions across the frontier were becoming more serious and more frequent, it was his duty to protect innocent colonial citizens from the depredations of an implacable and aggressive enemy. His case was not totally spurious. Haile Selassie's control over the outlying areas of his kingdom was far from complete, Eritrea had, indeed, been the victim of frequent and damaging attacks. It was obvious, however, that Mussolini's main object was not to protect his territories but to conquer and settle large tracts of, still better the whole of Abyssinia. "There has been talk of a compromise," he told De Bono, "but I have let it be understood that we shall not turn back for any price." He realised that this would inevitably involve a clash with, possibly even the complete severance of relations, with the League of Nations. "We may have to leave Geneva," he admitted. The prospect did not cause him grave concern. If it had been possible he would have preferred to avoid any such confrontation, but he was satisfied that, if Italy was condemned by or even expelled from the League, there would be no military consequences and the political and economic price would not be intolerably high.

The quicker his victory, the less likely it was that that the rest of the world would muster any effective opposition. It soon became apparent that the miracle of Adowa was not about to be repeated. The Abyssinians were less well prepared, the invading Italian army was larger and better armed than its hapless predecessor. The war was won quickly, boasted Mussolini, "by reason of our immense moral, spiritual and cultural superiority and of our crushing superiority in armaments and resources of every kind." The morality and the spirituality of the Italians may fairly be questioned, their military superiority was all too evident. Within a few days Adowa had been occupied and a triumphant monument erected on the site of Italy's past humiliation. It was not only the Italian army that proved itself superior, its air force freely ranged the skies without a trace of effective opposition. The luckless Abyssinians were bombed and strafed relentlessly. Not only were they attacked with high explosives, they were the victims of mustard gas dropped on them in barrels or sprayed as a lethal rain. In fact their use of gas probably cost the Italians more in terms of reputation than it gained them militarily: the image of a well-equipped Western power attacking under-armed and badly organised Africans left a bad taste; when to this was added the use of a weapon that was not merely barbarous but was specifically forbidden by international law, then Italy was indeed casting itself in the role of villain. But the use of gas certainly contributed to the Abyssinians' discomfiture and made their rapid defeat more certain.

* * *

The question remained what, if anything, the rest of the world was going to do. If it had not been for the existence of the League of Nations the answer would have been "Very little!" Great Britain and France were the only nations in Europe whose possible reactions caused the Italians serious concern and their own imperial record was hardly such as to encourage them to strike a boldly moral note when it came to denouncing Italian aggression in Africa. If they had been left to themselves they would have made disapproving noises and nothing more. Britain had investigated

the possibility of buying off the Italians by offering them territorial concessions in other parts of East Africa but that was as far
as they felt inclined to go. When it came to taking serious military
or even economic action to deter the aggressors, there was a
marked lack of enthusiasm. Britain and France, however, were
not left to themselves. Both countries, like Italy and Abyssinia,
were members of the League of Nations, and this meant that a
new and significant element was involved. From the point of view
of the world at large, it is the role that the League played or, more
accurately, failed to play in the Abyssinian war that lends significance to that impassioned yet essentially trivial conflict.

Since the United States had withdrawn from the League
towards the end of 1919, the organisation had limped on, still of
importance in the world but effectively dependent for its potency
on its European members. It had played a useful role in the settlement of several minor disputes but in effect was little more
than a mechanism in which the dominant powers – France and
Britain, with Italy a significant but still junior member of the
triumvirate – could find and impose solutions on the lesser
powers. For the other members, it was a forum in which it was
possible, almost obligatory, to air praiseworthy sentiments without any serious expectation that effective action would follow as
a result. "Friends of democracy, Buchmanites, women's societ-
ies, students' federations, Christian Scientists, Leagues of Youth,
anti-Fascist and anti-war associations for this or that good cause"
swarmed to Geneva, confident that they would find a sympathetic audience and not unduly depressed by the fact that little
practical action was likely to result from their expostulations.
A situation had not yet arisen in which two of the three great

powers were at loggerheads with each other or one of them behaved in a way that the other two thought unacceptable. When, or if, this did happen it was clear that the League would face a new and most challenging test. In October 1935 that moment arrived.

* * *

Nine months earlier the Abyssinian government had reported to the League that the Italians were massing their troops in Eritrea and that this could only be with a view to launching an attack on their neighbour. Unfortunately for them, the powerful French Foreign Minister, Pierre Laval, had little sympathy for independent African states and was well-disposed towards Fascist Italy. Anthony Eden, at that time Lord Privy Seal and the British minister most directly concerned with the affair, was equally unenthusiastic about any involvement of the League in Italy's African adventures. Neither government considered that any serious national interest was involved, both were more concerned about the increasing perils caused by German rearmanent and the excesses of the Nazi regime. They saw Italy as a potential ally against Germany; at the very least they were anxious to avoid the creation of a German–Italian axis. If the price that had to be paid for this was the acceptance of Italian claims on Abyssinia, the price was worth paying. Haile Selassie was urged to do nothing that might provoke his bellicose neighbours and to make whatever territorial concessions were necessary to buy them off.

Italy was not bought off; on the contrary, it was encouraged by what it saw as the tacit acquiescence of France and Britain in its African adventure. Within a few months it had destroyed the greater part of the Abyssinian army and occupied Addis Ababa. In Geneva the League of Nations watched impotently. Salvador de Madariaga y Rojo, chairman of the committee that had been set up to secure a peaceful end to the conflict, was instructed to mediate between the belligerents and to persuade them "within the framework of the League of Nations and in the spirit of the Covenant to bring about a prompt cessation of hostilities and the final restoration of peace". The sentiment was admirable but when it came to the point the spirit of the Covenant failed signally to make much impression on the Italian government. "Does collective security consist only in making platonic protests against the aggressor and addressing words of compassion to his victim?" demanded the Emperor. The short and brutal answer was that it did. Eden continued to protest that Britain was ready to join with fellow members of the League in applying further and more effective sanctions but he did singularly little to bring about any such denouement. When Abyssinian resistance finally collapsed the League was still professing its good intentions but, while deploring Italian misbehaviour, doing virtually nothing to check its aggression.

* * *

Was there, in fact, anything effective that could have been done? Could the League have acted in a way that would have saved Abyssinia? Theoretically Britain and France might have rallied the other countries of the League and have threatened military action against Italy. It would, indeed, have been no more than a threat – by the time any serious attack on Italy could have been launched Abyssinia would have been long conquered – but even so it might have acted as a deterrent. In practice, however, neither government seriously contemplated the possibility, nor did the Italians believe for a moment that they were likely to do so. As Czechoslovakia was soon to discover, the preservation of peace in Europe was the paramount concern of the French and British. In 1938 Neville Chamberlain was to plead how "horrible, fantastic, incredible" it was that Britain should be contemplating war "because of a quarrel in a far-away country between people of whom we know nothing". How much further away Abyssinia was than Czechoslovakia, how much less the British knew about its people. But military action was not the only option. Effective economic sanctions, in particular an embargo on the export of oil and other petroleum products to Italy, would have put the aggressor at a singular disadvantage. They would have taken some time to implement – one of the reasons for the precipitate action of the Italians was Mussolini's anxiety to get the worst of the fighting over before any effective opposition could be mounted – but if the League had acted promptly they could still have caused grave inconvenience to the Italians and might conceivably have led them to call off their operations. Promptitude was not, however, a feature of British or French policy-making at the time, and the more effective the sanctions might have been, the greater the reluctance to impose them. Nor, even if the European powers had acted swiftly and effectively, was it by any means certain that the rest of the world would have followed suit. The British government, Anthony Eden insisted, were in favour of imposing an oil embargo "if other members of the League were prepared to do likewise", but he did little to rally support for such a measure and dithered unconvincingly until it was too late for even the most emphatic action to make any real difference.

To be fair to him, he had other, more urgent preoccupations. In March 1936, when the League of Nations was busily – perhaps "lethargically" would be a better word – discussing the possibility of an oil embargo, German troops marched into the Rhineland. Britain and France were brutally reminded where the most potent threat to world peace was to be found; Italy and its African adventures suddenly seemed something of a sideshow. The need to keep Italy as an ally , or at least to prevent the formation of too firm a German–Italian axis, became of paramount importance. By then it was anyway too late to take any effective action to help Haile Selassie; the invasion of the Rhineland ensured that the tears which were shed at Abyssinia's funeral were cursory and fleeting. It remained only to sweep under the carpet the ashes of the League's good intentions. Eden was one of the more honest when it came to admitting how complete its failure had been. "Not one of us here present," he declared in a speech in Geneva, "can contemplate with any measure of satisfaction, the circumstances in which this assembly meets on this occasion. It is an occasion painful for us all." Painful, above all, for Abyssinia.

NOTES FOR FURTHER READING

Evelyn Waugh's *Waugh in Abyssinia* (London 1936) is the liveliest and most entertaining personal account of the war in Abyssinia. George Martelli's *Italy Against the World* (London 1937) is the first, by no means unsuccessful, attempt to write an objective account of the campaign. Pietro Badoglio's *The War in Abyssinia* (London 1937), with a foreword by Mussolini, unabashedly presents the Italian version of events. Among more recent studies John Gooch's *Mussolini and his Generals* (Cambridge 2007) lucidly explains the background to Italian militarism and provides a succinct and scholarly analysis of the war itself.

16

THE GREAT PURGE

1936

"Tranquil" is not a word that can readily be applied to Russia in the twentieth century. The Great Terror of 1936 to 1938 was not an isolated phenomenon: terror was a state of mind to which the Russians were all too well accustomed. It was, however, more terrible than anything that had come before or was to come.

***

By the end of 1932 Joseph Stalin had successfully imposed something close to absolutist rule on Soviet Russia with a thoroughness that made the despotic rule of the Tsars seem almost like a vision of relaxed and consensual government. The peasants, intensely conservative, passionately wedded to their own patches of soil, had been brutally crushed, at the cost, perhaps, of some two million lives. M. N. Ryutin, potentially the most effective obstacle in Stalin's march to supreme power, had been expelled from the Party and arrested; if Stalin had had his way Ryutin's execution would have followed within a few days or weeks, but though the dictator was in most ways omnipotent, he did not feel that he could totally ignore the sensibilities of some of his more squeamish followers.

РАБОТНИКИ НКВД ПРИ ДОПРОСАХ „ВРАГОВ НАРОДА"
ПРИМЕНЯЛИ СТАРОРУССКУЮ ПЫТКУ — ДЫБУ...

УЗАКОНЕННЫЙ И.СТАЛИНЫМ И ГЕНЕРАЛЬНЫМ ПРОКУРОРОМ СССР А.ВЫШИНСК-
ИМ, ДОПРОС 3-Й СТЕПЕНИ ПОЗВОЛЯЛ ВЫКОЛАЧИВАТЬ ЛЮБЫЕ ПОКАЗАНИЯ   У
„ВРАГА НАРОДА" НА СЕБЯ И ДРУГИХ ЛИЦ, И МНОГИЕ, ЧТОБЫ ИЗБАВИТЬ СЕБЯ ОТ
ДАЛЬНЕЙШИХ ПЫТОК „ ПРИЗНАВАЛИСЬ" В ШПИОНАЖЕ, ДИВЕРСИИ, ЗАГОВО-
РЕ И Т.Д., СОЗНАТЕЛЬНО ШЛИ ПОД РАССТРЕЛ В УБОЙНОМ ЦЕХЕ УФУ НКВД...

"Third degree interrogation" from *Drawings from the Gulag* by Danzig
Baldaev, an artist who worked as a warder at Kresty prison in Leningrad.
See p.301 for the translation of the caption.

In the years that followed Stalin applied himself to reinforcing his already immensely powerful position, until such time as no-one, however influential, however well placed in the Communist establishment, could effectively challenge his authority. One of the very few who could seriously be considered a rival was Sergei Kirov; master of the Communist organisation in Leningrad and an orator of spellbinding ability. Kirov was murdered in December 1934: to the ostentatious grief of Stalin who was almost certainly responsible for the killing. Kirov's closest ally, Borisov, died in a convenient motor car accident within a few days of his friend's murder: no-one can prove that the "accident" was contrived but the fact that Stalin was a beneficiary of the mishap makes it seem all too likely that he had a hand in it. Kirov's murder was made the excuse for a wave of arrests and summary trials: not even the most farcical of trials was thought necessary to justify the expulsion of many thousands of potential dissidents from Leningrad and other cities to Siberia.

To the more optimistic Russians it seemed that this orgy of blood-letting, whether or not it had been justifiable or necessary, had achieved its end. By early 1935 the state seemed secure. Surely now there could be some relaxation; the ordinary law-abiding citizen need not continue to feel himself perpetually under threat? Such optimism did not take account of the paranoid suspicions of the dictator. In Stalin's eyes the state was far from secure; not merely was constant vigilance required but the hydra of counter-revolution was rearing its venomous heads in every direction and must not only be countered but anticipated and forestalled. Quite how far Stalin himself believed in the reality of his nightmares or how far he consciously nurtured them as an excuse for unimaginable atrocities is a question that probably even he would not have been able adequately to answer: from the point of view of the Russian citizen it was of little importance; the fact of what was happening was enough.

1935 and 1936 saw no easing of repression; on the contrary, they were marked by an inexorable tightening of the laws, the imposition of ever harsher penalties not only on those who had been shown to be disloyal but on those who might be suspected of disloyalty, even on those who might be suspected of one day contemplating disloyalty. No-one was safe: it seemed that even to exist was sufficient to pose a potential threat to the state that justified imprisonment and, as often as not, subsequent execution. In April 1935 the death penalty for treason was extended to children as young as twelve; three months later it was enacted that relations of those who had fled abroad were liable to imprisonment or exile to Siberia, even though it could be shown that they had no prior knowledge of their kinsmen's intentions. Impeccable loyalty, a proven record of service to the state, seemed only to make arrest and conviction more probable.

Viewed from the secure fastness of a Western democracy in the twenty-first century it is difficult to understand why so many people allowed themselves meekly to be obliterated in this fashion. Even those who were responsible for organising and implementing the processes of arrest, trial and execution must have realised that they themselves were likely next to fall victim, that nobody was safe, that only the destruction of the Communist monster could stop it devouring those who served it as well as those who opposed or were believed to oppose it. Perhaps they deluded themselves that they would prove to be in some way immune, perhaps they felt that they were caught up in a mighty tide that offered no possibility of escape. In any case, wave upon wave of largely blameless individuals submitted themselves to trial on charges that were often patently preposterous and made only the most half-hearted efforts to defend themselves, even though they knew that the price they would pay would be exile if they were lucky, execution if they were not.

The first set-piece trial of this current series began in mid-August 1936. Grigori Zinoviev, once one of Stalin's closest associates and a member of the original Politburo, was the most eminent among the accused. He was charge with forming a terrorist organisation that plotted to murder Stalin and other leading figures in the Soviet Government. He elected to plead guilty; allegedly on the understanding that, if he did so, his life would be spared. If such a promise was ever made, it was quickly broken: within a few hours of the sentence being passed, Zinoviev had been shot. It was not until 1988, in the period of *perestroika*, that he was finally absolved of any wrong-doing.

Some may have hoped that his downfall and execution would provide the high point of the Terror. Stalin had demonstrated that nobody was safe, that nobody could hope even to contemplate disloyalty without incurring the fearful vengeance of the State. It was surely unnecessary to gild the lily, or, rather, to drown in its own blood whatever vestige of counter-revolution might remain?

If such optimists existed they were quickly disabused. Stalin's suspicions were so paranoid and his determination to destroy any real or imaginary threats before they had any chance of destroying him was so all-consuming, that it was inevitable that Zinoviev's trial should prove only a curtain-raiser for the worse that was to come. That trial itself had pointed the way forward. Whether under duress or in an unavailing effort to save themselves, Zinoviev and his associates had sought to share their guilt with, most notably, Nikolai Bukharin, editor of the Communist Party newspaper *Pravda*, and Alexei Rykov, a moderate who had been Deputy Chairman to Lenin and at one time Premier of the Soviet Union.

These were big fish indeed: their arrest and trial for treason, followed by their execution on 15 March, 1938, was terrifying proof, both of the absolute power of Stalin and of the ruthlessness with which he would maintain it.

There had been only one centre of power which it had seemed possible might remain independent of the Communist Party and, conceivably, even intervene to check its excesses: the Red Army. Many of the most prominent and successful soldiers – notably Marshal Tukhachevsky, who though himself of aristocratic lineage had notably revolutionary tendencies – were themselves Communists or Communist sympathisers, but even these were for the most part moderate in their views and had little sympathy for the excesses of the political leadership. There is no doubt that elements among them were disposed to intervene, even to organise a coup that would have suppressed the Communist Party and imposed, temporarily at least, some form of military rule. When it came to the point, however, the will was lacking. The military leaders failed to strike while the iron was hot and were, in due course, struck themselves. In July 1936 the first blow fell: a general who had been vociferously and unwisely critical of Stalin was arrested. Possibly if the Army had reacted forcibly at that point they could still have prevailed: though by now firmly entrenched, the Party still did not command the instinctive reverence of the Russian people. Instead, they let it happen, and with every subsequent encroachment upon civil liberties it became more certain that they would never react effectively. To a remarkable extent the Army presided over its own elimination as an effective political force; the wonder was that it did not preside over its own elimination as an effective military force as well. That the Red Army would have provided more effective opposition to the German advance in 1941 if its officer class had not been purged so ruthlessly over the preceding years can hardly be doubted; that the Red Army was still an enormously effective fighting force was proved by the proud record of its resistance and eventual victory.

The Communist Party never became – by definition, never could become – a democratic movement tolerating, even welcoming opposition. The Purges may have petered out, but the instinct to purge would endure. If, in 1939 and 1940, it had not become increasingly apparent that, in Nazi Germany, the Russian Government confronted a danger far more menacing and more immediate than anything that could possibly emerge from within its own borders, it is at least possible that the Purges would have been resumed with fresh and fearful force. Russia's war with Germany was hideously expensive in lives and materials; it devastated vast areas of the country, but at least it gave the Russian people and leadership something to think about other than its internal dissension. The history of post-war Russia has not been one of impeccable peace and prosperity but at least the horror of the Purges has never been renewed.

NOTES FOR FURTHER READING

Robert Conquest's *The Great Terror* is the classic text. It was originally published in 1968 and reissued as *The Great Terror: A Reassessment* (London 1990). Simon Sebag Montefiore's *Stalin: The Court of the Red Tsar* (London 2003) is informative and immensely readable.

17

GUERNICA

1937

At 4.00 p.m. on Monday, 4 March, 1937, the first wave of German planes from the Condor Legion began to drop their bombs on the Spanish town of Guernica. A new form of warfare had been initiated. It was to find a dreadful echo in Coventry, Dresden and hundreds of other cities and towns around the world.

* * *

It was the bad luck of Guernica that it was chosen to be the target for this overwhelming assault. The Germans, indeed, had no compelling reason to be involved at all in what should have been an exclusively domestic conflict. Spain was more than capable of making trouble for itself without outside assistance. It was a nation traditionally prone to turbulence and disorder and the first decades of the twentieth century offered little indication that things had changed. By keeping out of the First World War Spain had, to some extent, strengthened its position in Europe, but the impact of the disease known, because of its apparent origins, as "Spanish Flu" and the country's immensely expensive involvement in the Moroccan War, cost Spain dear, and when the Great Depression struck, the country was reduced to near-

Aerial view of the ruins of Guernica.

bankruptcy. The on-the-whole well-intentioned but inept dictatorship of General Primo de Rivera signally failed to restore prosperity and in 1931 a crushing electoral victory for the left led to the flight of the King and the establishment of a republic. An uneasy coalition of liberals, socialists, anarchists and communists temporarily came to power but it failed fully to establish itself and in 1933 the right, depending heavily for its authorit on the backing of the Church, found itself once more in control. Moderation, tolerance, compromise – concepts intrinsic to successful democratic government – were hard to find in Spain in the 1930s. Neither left nor right was prepared to make concessions, let alone work harmoniously together. Any move towards the right seemed inevitably to tend towards the authoritarian and the reactionary, any move to the left, to damaging strikes and anarchy. Of these two displeasing alternatives, the majority of Spaniards were probably disposed to favour the left, but what they wanted most of all was stability and a quiet life.

General Francisco Franco, Chief of the Spanish General Staff, felt that was something for which he was uniquely qualified. When a Popular Front coalition won the election in February 1936 he decided that enough was more than enough and attempted to introduce martial law. He was before his time: the coup failed and he was dispatched to a post where it was felt that he could do no harm – Military Governor of the Canary Islands. It proved to be only a jumping-off point from which he could launch his next attempt to assume power. Spain in his absence became ever more disorderly: right and left vied with each other in inept misgovernment, once more the Army felt that it was its duty to intervene. In July Franco took control of Spanish

Morocco; from there he proclaimed that the anarchy in Spain could no longer be endured and that martial law was now in force.

He took it for granted that, with the army loyally behind him, he would have little trouble in imposing his authority. It turned out, however, that the Left was far more capable of fighting its own corner than it had been of administering the country. The twenty-three-year-old Communist journalist Dolores Ibárruri – *La Pasionaria*, as she became generally known – proclaimed that the country was "shaking with indignation, faced with these heartless men who, with fire and terror, want to plunge popular and democratic Spain into an inferno of terror". "They shall not pass!" she trumpeted, and "*no pasarán*" became the rallying cry of the legitimate government against the Fascist insurgents. And they did not pass – or not at first, at least. Spain became embroiled in a hideously destructive civil war which raged for the rest of 1936 and throughout 1937. It was Franco's army that proved the more effective but it was far from being a walkover and there were times at which the legitimate government seemed to be reasserting its authority.

On the whole the British people favoured the cause of the legitimate government. It did not look like that to George Orwell, however. "In the most mean, cowardly, hypocritical way," he wrote, "the British ruling class did all they could to hand Spain over to Franco and the Nazis." The charge was not one that the Conservative Prime Minister, Stanley Baldwin, would have accepted. He had no intention of allowing his country to be drawn into the conflict: "non-intervention" was the order of the day. Many individuals, however, journeyed to Spain to join in the fighting.

Most of them joined the republican army – the army of the legitimate government – but some supported Franco and it cannot have been unheard of for Briton to confront Briton across the battle lines.

This was strictly private enterprise, however – the British government deplored what they saw as an ill-judged escapade and did what they could to check it. The situation was very different in Germany and Italy, whose governments overtly supported Franco's Nationalist regime. Hermann Göring, First World War fighter pilot and Commander-in-Chief of the German Luftwaffe, was particularly pleased to give his fledgling air force a chance to try out its weapons and hone its skills in somebody else's conflict. He had originally volunteered to provide a few transport aircraft which would help carry Franco's troops from North Africa to Spain; ground troops followed – though in relatively small numbers – and by the early summer of 1937, the fighters and bombers of the Condor Legion were making an immensely important contribution to the Fascist cause. The heartland of the country was by now in Franco's hands, resistance was confined largely to the Mediterranean coast and the Basque provinces to the north. It was in the Basque country that the German aircraft, permitted as they were to range the skies without any significant opposition, made their most important contribution. Bombers under the command of Lieutenant Colonel Wolfram von Richthofen, a cousin of the celebrated Manfred von Richthofen, the "Red Baron", who had been a hero of the German air force in the First World War, closely supported the rebel army in its advance towards Bilbao. By April 26 almost the only town of any size or strategic importance left between the advancing Nationalists and Bilbao was Guernica. Von Richt-hofen decreed that it must be eliminated.

There were good military reasons for this decision, though Guernica itself was by no means an obvious target: its only bar-racks lay well outside the town as also did a munitions factory which, anyway, was hardly large enough to justify a raid. It was, however, from the point of view of its inhabitants at least, in the wrong place; it was an important communications centre through which government troops needed regularly to move and was thus a compelling target for the Germans. It was also a town of particular significance to the Basques – their spiritual if not their political capital. But the Germans first and foremost decided to attack it because they wanted to attack *somewhere* and Guernica was conveniently to hand. They wanted to satisfy themselves and to demonstrate to the rest of the world that they could and would obliterate from the air any city which got in their way. To defy the might of Germany was to court extinction: it was Guernica today, tomorrow it might be Paris or London. The Luftwaffe was a new and dreadful force which would trans-form the nature of twentieth-century war: over Guernica it came of age.

There was no reason to anticipate the holocaust that was to come. In the early evening of March 4 a solitary German aeroplane flew over the centre of the town and dropped three bombs. It had been a market day and the streets were crowded but the bombs did little damage and the inhabitants hopefully assumed that that was the end of it. Their optimism was short-lived: within a few minutes a squadron of seven more bombers was overhead, then came another six; squadron after squadron processed over Guernica, unloading their cargoes of 250-kilo-gram splinter bombs and thermite incendiary bombs. The pilots came in low, knowing that Guernica possessed no anti-aircraft guns that could seriously discommode them and that the Republican air force, in so far as it existed, was nowhere near the scene. When the panic-stricken citizens tried to escape the bombs by fleeing the town, German and Italian fighters machine-gunned them, killing hundreds and wounding many more. By the time the last wave of attackers had cleared the scene, some three hours after the first bombs had fallen, more than sixteen hundred citizens of Guernica were dead. "The most appalling air raid ever known," read the Reuters report: "I have seen many ghastly sights in Spain in the last six months," wrote Noël Monks in the *Daily Express*, "but none more terrible than the annihilation of the ancient Basque capital of Guernica by Franco's bombing planes." It was not the first time that defenceless cities had been ravaged from the air – Dacca, Baghdad, Damascus, Shanghai had all been earlier victims – but the destruction of Guernica was by far the most comprehensive and, perhaps equally important, it was the most vividly and widely reported. Guernica shocked the world. Among those who felt outrage was a Spanish painter living in exile in France: his name was Pablo Picasso.

* * *

By 1937 Picasso was probably the best-known painter in the world. "Best-known" does not necessarily mean most respected. Though the howls of derision that had hailed the breakthrough into Cubism which he and Georges Braque had pioneered some

thirty years before had by now died down, he was still a controversial figure, derided by philistines and viewed with some
caution by the more traditional elements of the art establishment. Politically, he was not yet a Communist but he was known
to be far to the Left and to number many Communists among
his friends and associates. Yet he was not blindly committed to
the cause; from his mother he had received horrifying reports
of vandalised churches and murdered nuns and he knew that
atrocities were being committed by Nationalists and Communists alike. "Guernica" was painted more to illustrate the horrors
of war than to condemn the iniquities of one side or the other.

1937 had been chosen by the French government as the year
for a great international exhibition to be held in Paris. The official Spanish government was anxious that its pavilion should be
one of the most conspicuous; nothing was more likely to attract
attention than a major canvas by Spain's most celebrated painter.
Given the circumstances it was likely, if not inevitable, that that
painting would possess a stong political content. "My whole life
as an artist has been nothing more than a continuous struggle
against reaction and the death of art," Picasso wrote in May
1937. By his contribution to the Exhibition he intended clearly to
express "my abhorrence of the military caste which has sunk
Spain in an ocean of pain and death". If the subject had not been
Guernica it would have been another of the many tragic incidents in that peculiarly savage war, and almost certainly Picasso
would have chosen one which featured the sufferings of civilians
at the hands of soldiers of the right. The peculiar horror of the
subject, however, not merely captured Picasso's imagination
but inspired a creative fury which impelled him to work with

phenomenal speed and concentration. "Guernica" is a huge painting – eleven feet six inches by twenty-five feet eight; Picasso worked on it for less than two months; effectively it was created in six weeks, between May 1, when he made his first cursory sketch, and the middle of June, when he decided that it was ready for delivery to the Spanish Pavilion, in front of the just-completed Palais de Chaillot on the bank of the Seine. Physically, the Spanish pavilion was over-shadowed by its massively portentous neighbour representing Nazi Germany; it was more than anything else Picasso's "Guernica" which ensured that it was the Spanish pavilion which was the more widely reported on and remembered.

Not that "Guernica" was immediately and universally acclaimed. José Maria Ucclay, the Basque painter, was by no means alone in denouncing it as "one of the poorest things ever produced in the world. It has no sense of composition, or for that matter anything... it's just 7 x 3 metres of pornography!" In the *Spectator* Anthony Blunt complained that the painting was "disillusioning . . . It is not an act of public mourning, but the expression of a private brain-storm which gives no evidence that Picasso has realised the political significance of Guernica." A feeling that "Guernica" was wilfully, self-indulgently obscure and that its title had merely been tacked onto it by an artist who wanted to cash in on the outrage caused by events in Spain was held by many people who knew little or nothing of Picasso's work as well as by some who were better qualified to comment. Le Corbusier, one of the most renowned and adventurous architects in the world, dismissed it as ugly and inconsiderable. "'Guernica' saw only the backs of our visitors," he wrote, "for they were repelled by it."

But for every serious critic who belittled Picasso's achievement there was another who praised it ecstatically. Herbert Read, editor of the influential *Burlington Magazine*, was one of the more established of Picasso's champions. "Guernica", he wrote, was a religious picture, painted "with the same degree of fervour that inspired Grünewald and the master of the Avignon *Pietà*, Van Eyck and Bellini". Picasso's symbols were deliberately banal, "like the symbols of Homer, Dante, Cervantes. For it is only when the widest commonplace is infused with the intensest passion that a great work of art, transcending all schools and categories, is born; and being born, lives immortally."

Live immortally? There must have been some doubt in 1937 whether it would live at all. As the painting was being finished Picasso had sold it to the Republic of Spain for 150,000 francs (a sum he later donated to the Spanish Refugee Relief Campaign). Most of the contents of the Spanish Pavilion were dispatched to Valencia, where they fell victim to Spain's increasingly ferocious civil war, and there seemed no reason why "Guernica" should be more fortunate. For some reason, however, it was set aside and joined the "Desmoiselles d'Avignon", another of Picasso's most celebrated masterpieces, in the painter's studio in Paris.

It did not long remain there. Early in 1938 it joined paintings by Braque, Laurens and Matisse in a tour of the main Scandinavian cities; later in the same year the mural, with many of the preparatory drawings, was sent to London for display at the New Burlington Galleries. From there it moved to the Whitechapel Art Gallery, centre point of an exhibition designed to advance the cause of the National Joint Committee for Spanish Relief. Clement Attlee, Leader of the Labour Party and seven years later

to serve as Prime Minister in the first British post-war government, spoke at the official opening. He was hardly an obvious
candidate for the role of champion of contemporary art but he
rose bravely to the occasion and predicted that the horrors which
Picasso portrayed on his canvas were only a foretaste of what the
Fascists of Germany and Italy would soon be unleashing on
Europe.

What was to be its final resting place? Picasso hoped that it
would one day be Madrid but there could be no question of it
going to Spain at a time when Franco was clearly well on the way
to winning control of the whole country. Instead, it crossed the
Atlantic for an exhibition in the United States designed to raise
money for Spanish relief. Under the auspices of a group of spon-
sors which included such diverse celebrities as Albert Einstein,
Ernest Hemingway and Thomas Mann, the painting toured the
country before returning to New York in November 1939 to
feature in a retrospective exhibition of Picasso's work at the
Museum of Modern Art (M.O.M.A.). Once again, the critical
reception was mixed but public interest was passionate and sustained. Sixty thousand people visited M.O.M.A. and it was above
all to see "Guernica", or at least to be able to say that they had
seen "Guernica", that they took the trouble to make the trip.

And in New York, for more than forty years, it remained.
While its creator spent uneasy years in German-occupied Paris,
his most famous painting gathered ever greater celebrity in
the United States. Quite why Picasso chose to remain in France
is obscure – "inertia" was his own explanation. Once, it is said,
a German officer pushed a reproduction of "Guernica" under
Picasso's nose. "You did that, didn't you?" he asked. "No," Picasso

replied, "You did!" Certainly Picasso never wavered in his belief that Fascism was the most virulent and destructive force of the twentieth century and that, in painting "Guernica", he had been denouncing not merely a particularly brutal incident in a particularly brutal war but a whole philosophy of evil. "Guernica" was a trumpet call in the battle against totalitarianism; the fact that it was also a singularly beautiful and important work of art is something that will appear to some much less, to some much more important.

Picasso did not live to see "Guernica" find what will surely be its final home in Spain. He died in 1973, while Franco still survived after thirty-four years of dictatorial rule. It was not till September 1981, with Franco dead and democracy restored, that the painting was installed in the expensively renovated Casón del Buen Retiro in Madrid. "Never in its history has 'Guernica' been displayed so beautifully or so entirely to its advantage," wrote Douglas Cooper, eminent art historian and close friend of the painter. By that time the town of Guernica had itself been restored. Beginning in 1940, a massive programme of reconstruction had been undertaken, seeking not, as was later to be the case in Warsaw, to renovate the old town but to lay out a new town with parks, landscaped gardens, a spacious marketplace, lengthy arcades. The Guernica that Franco built was undoubtedly better planned and more convenient than the town it replaced: whether those who were left of the original inhabitants were thereby consoled for the loss of their former homes seems more doubtful. "A visit to a place like Guernica," wrote Franco's apologist, the Marqués de Santa María del Villar, "is, we believe, edifying and greatly instructive – a journey that is necessary for all Spaniards, particularly our youth. How it teaches us of the distinctions between the destructive labour of Communism and the restoration of Franco's Spain." The Fascist line was that the destruction of Guernica had been the work, not of German or Italian bombers, but of communists ready to sacrifice their fellow countrymen so as to score a propaganda victory. The lie, for a time, gained credence among the more gullible but the facts were too patent to be indefinitely ignored. The Guernica destroyed by Fascist bombers, the Guernica commemorated by Picasso's terrifying vision, was established for ever as the first manifestation of a new and terrible form of warfare. In 1937 it was unique; within a few years it would become a commonplace.

NOTES FOR FURTHER READING

For the raid on Guernica as an incident in the Spanish Civil War one cannot do better than read Hugh Thomas's masterly *The Spanish Civil War* (revised edition, London 1977). Picasso's treatment of the event must have been as much written about as any painting of the twentieth century. Among the books I found particularly interesting were Gijs van Hansbergen's *Guernica* (London 2004), Russell Martin's *Picasso's War* (London 2003) and Anthony Blunt's *Picasso's Guernica* (London 1969). Of the many biographies of Picasso, that by Roland Penrose (London 1955) probably remains the most attractive to the general reader. Eberhard Fisch, in *Guernica by Picasso* (Lewisburg 1988) provides a most exhaustive analysis of the painting in all its detail.

18

JAPAN AND CHINA AT WAR

1937

The Marco Polo Bridge – which has nothing to do with Marco Polo except that he may possibly once have visited its predecessor – is to be found some twelve miles to the south-west of Peking. In July 1937 it marked the border between areas occupied by the Japanese North China Garrison Army, which had invaded Manchuria in 1931, and the Chinese 29th Army. On the evening of July 7, a desultory skirmish began between the two forces. Something similar had often happened in the past without anything more serious transpiring but this time, for some reason, both sides seemed resolved to push the matter further. A skirmish became a battle, a battle became a war. It was to take eight years and fifteen million lives for the conflict to be resolved.

* * *

Though there was no reason why this particular incident should have proved so important, it had for many years seemed likely if not certain that Japan and China would one day come to war. Japan was, of course, far the smaller, with a population of some seventy million against China's more than five hundred million, but it was also the better organised and disciplined, a

A baby abandoned at Shanghai's South Station, 28 August 1937.

fully functioning nation while China was little more than a loose federation of frequently squabbling provinces. China, remarked Nigel Ronald of the British Foreign Office, "is not a unit susceptible of clear definition, it is rather a vague concept sanctified by long usage". Japan, on the other hand, was quite as much sanctified by long usage but was very far from being "a vague concept". Since the Americans, with what they must subsequently have considered ill-judged zeal, had in the mid-nineteenth century forced Japan to emerge from the feudal chrysalis in which it had long lingered, the Japanese had concluded that, if you could not beat them, you had better join or, at least, emulate them. They had modernised with startling speed and efficiency and by 1900 could boast the most developed industry and the most formidable army of any Asian power. Inevitably, their new-found strength led to tension in their relationship with their mighty but mismanaged neighbour, China. The two countries first clashed in Korea, traditionally a fief of the Chinese empire but by the 1890s an easy target for any more virile invader. Japan then turned its attention to Manchuria, where Russia, without actually claiming the province as its own, was accustomed to exercising predominant power. The crumbling Tsarist empire had more than enough problems to preoccupy it in other parts of the world; it was quickly defeated in the Russo-Japanese War of 1904–5, and, in the Treaty that followed, mediated by the American President, Theodore Roosevelt, Russia agreed to evacuate Manchuria, leaving Japan the dominant power in East Asia and in effective control of South Manchuria. Its ambitions and growing power alarmed the West, but though the United States, if encouraged, might have been ready to intervene in one way or another, the British were, not unreasonably, preoccupied by the growing probability of war in Europe and insisted that, if any action were to be taken, it should be through the League of Nations. Predictably this ensured that no effective action was taken and no significant pressure was brought on Japan to curb its ambitions. Anthony Eden, the British Foreign Secretary, comforted himself with the reflection that Japan was fundamentally in a weak position, because of "the overshadowing presence of Russia, lack of financial strength and the enormous latent and elastic power of resistance which China possesses".

For China, things went from bad to worse. Revolution in 1911 had not led to the development of a new and virile democracy but to chaotic disintegration which justified Nigel Ronald's contemptuous dismissal of its national status. In the mid-1920s the country was riven between two great power groups: the Nationalists, under Chiang Kai-shek and the Communists, under Mao Zedong. The conflict was savage and unrelenting: neither party can be said finally to have won but by the early 1930s Chiang was established, in the eyes of the West at least, as *de facto* if not *de jure* ruler of what was now the Chinese Republic.

The most obvious beneficiary of the chaos in China had been neither the Communists nor the Nationalists but the Japanese. Chiang, disastrously underestimating the threat that they posed, believed that it was his Communist fellow countrymen, not the Japanese, who were most to be feared when it came to planning China's future. "I give you my word that, within three years, we shall have beaten the Japanese to their knees!" he told a group of students.

His remark has not been precisely dated but it cannot have

been long after he made it that he began to wonder whether his confidence was justified. Even more than Europe and the United States, Japan had been a victim of the economic crash of 1928 and 1929, but, unlike most of the other victims, it had reacted by resorting to an even more militaristic and violently authoritarian regime. The Manchurian escapade of the 1930s had been not so much an imperialistic adventure as a desperate move by an embattled and financially hard-pressed government to find somewhere which it could exploit economically and where it could export its over-crowded population. When the Japanese found that they had got away with it, that the Chinese, though not condoning the occupation of Manchuria, did not seem disposed to launch a major war in its defence, they were encouraged to push things further, in particular to cast covetous eyes on the vast and economically all-important city of Shanghai.

In so doing they turned what had hitherto been an all-Asian affair into a potential confrontation with the West. Since the end of the first Opium War in the 1840s Shanghai had been the most international of Chinese cities, perhaps the most international city in the world. Two "concession zones" – predominantly French and British respectively – were effectively independent entities; the United States also established a strong and rapidly growing presence. Waves of White Russians and Russian Jews arrived in the nineteenth century; a further thirty thousand Jewish refugees fled Europe for Shanghai in the 1930s. By 1937 it was not merely the world's fifth largest city and home to nearly a hundred thousand foreigners, but Asia's most important financial centre. Not for nothing was it known as the "Great Athens of China" – though the Greeks would hardly have been likely to accept such a designation for a city so exclusively devoted to trade and the acquisition of vast fortunes.

The Japanese had no wish to kill a goose that laid so many golden eggs. They behaved with circumspection. Ironically, it was Chinese aircraft which, in a bungled attempt to destroy Japanese warships anchored on the Huangpu river, scattered their bombs on the centre of the city and killed more than a thousand civilians, including some in the International Settlements. Ferocious fighting followed – large parts of the city were in fact hardly touched by the war but the economic consequences were catastrophic. "Like a nightmare octopus flinging cruel tentacles around its helpless victims," the *North China Daily News* told its readers, "the local hostilities are slowly strangling Shanghai." The British writer Christopher Isherwood visited the city with his friend W. H. Auden some months after the fighting was over. He had only recently witnessed the Spanish Civil War so he was well used to devastation, but he was still appalled by what he saw as the "stark, frightful wilderness which was once the Chinese city". The Japanese, after they had completed its occupation, made desultory efforts to patch up some of the damage, but Shanghai was never wholly to regain its pre-eminence and no serious reconstruction was to be set in train until long after the final defeat of the Japanese in 1945.

* * *

The Japanese, in fact, were by no means so unequivocally belligerent in the mid-1930s as their subsequent history might lead one to expect. Ishiwara Kanji, for instance, the Chief of the

General Staff Operations Division and one of the most significant figures in the modernisation of Japan's army, believed that an out-and-out war between East and West was in the end inevitable and that therefore any conflict with China was, at the best, an irrelevance and, at the worst, a disastrous diversion from what should have been a united crusade. "Not one soldier is going to be sent to China while I am alive," he boasted, but, when it came to the point, he proved unable to divert the main thrust of Japanese aggression and, far from dying, played a significant role in its execution. On the whole, it was the Japanese soldiers who doubted the wisdom of the foray into China, the politicians who urged it on. When the General Staff argued the case against war the Navy Minister retorted: "If the General Staff has no confidence in the government, then either the General Staff must resign or the government must resign." To no-one's surprise, the General Staff did not take advantage of this invitation: no-one resigned and the military machine cranked reluctantly forwards. There were not many Japanese who would have stated openly that they sought war with China, perhaps not even many who felt privately that this must or should be the final conclusion, yet by their behaviour they made it inevitable that this must one day happen. It came about that that one day was 7 July, 1937.

* * *

The incident at the Marco Polo Bridge could have occurred at any one of a hundred places. Over the previous week tensions had been noticeably rising. There seems no reason to believe that either side was exclusively or even primarily responsible. "Rumors have been current in Peiping . . . of possible disorders being created by disgruntled Chinese or Japanese nationals . . ." reported an American diplomat. It would have been hard to find a single Chinese or Japanese national who could have been described as entirely gruntled. The situation was one of a cold, or even tepid war bound soon to erupt into a hot one. In so far as there was any one individual who was responsible for deciding the place and time at which the eruption took place, it was the Chinese Nationalist commander, Chiang Kai-shek. Against the advice of most of his staff officers he concluded that this was not just one more trivial skirmish but was the preamble to a major Japanese offensive designed to conquer still more Chinese territory, perhaps even to destroy China's military capability for once and for all. "This is the turning point for existence or obliteration," he wrote in his diary. Some of his advisers argued that this was not the moment for a serious confrontation: in two years, perhaps, China would have built up its forces to a level at which they could confront the Japanese with some hope of success. On the contrary, Chiang retorted, however much China might build up its strength, Japan would do so more rapidly. Whatever imbalance there was between the two sides could only worsen to China's disadvantage. Better to strike now while China was still in with a chance.

For a time it seemed as if he might be, if not right, then at least not extravagantly wrong. After a few weeks of fierce fighting things seemed to be settling down. At one point the local Chinese and Japanese commanders even announced that a ceasefire had been agreed. But the news that substantial Chinese reinforcements were being moved north to the area of tension caused a sharp reaction in Tokyo. "Our strenuous efforts to reach an amicable settlement of the North China incident have to all appearances failed," declared Prince Fumimaro Konoe, the recently appointed Japanese Prime Minister. Left to himself, Konoe would probably nevertheless have temporised, have made conciliatory noises and done his best to ensure that the ceasefire held. But he was not left to himself: belligerent voices in his Cabinet demanded that the Japanese should strike while they still held the advantage; the military commanders, hitherto cautious, now rallied behind those who believed that only an immediate recourse to battle could save their position in China.

* * *

And so what might have been just one more skirmish – a skirmish which, because of the powers involved, would have been on a massive scale but a skirmish for all that – turned into all-out war.

Preoccupied as they were with their own concerns, the European powers took only a detached interest in these proceedings. The British chargé d'affaires in Tokyo maintained that the Japanese had not wanted the Marco Polo Bridge incident, still less did they want to see it escalate out of control. On the whole his view was accepted in London: of the two parties involved, China, it was felt, had been the more provocative. The British government was prepared to intervene, at least to the extent of making a joint approach with the United States, offering their services as an intermediary. It was the Americans who baulked, fearing that any such approach would lead to accusations that the West was ganging up on Japan. Instead they proposed that Britain and the United States should proceed along "parallel but independent lines" – a policy that effectively ensured that they did not proceed along any lines at all. The result was that it was once more the League of Nations that was charged with restoring peace, or at least with providing a forum in which some settlement might be worked out. The League proved no more effective than it had been in settling the dispute between Bolivia and Paraguay. Neither side can be said conclusively to have "won" the war between China and Japan, but the League of Nations was unequivocally the loser. As much as anyone, it was the British who were to blame for this debacle. They insisted that the League should not take any significant action unless the full co-operation of the United States was first secured. Neville Chamberlain stated formally that he was opposed to any economic boycott of Japan: he was, he said, "most anxious to avoid the position which had been reached with Italy over Abyssinia". He was prepared to condemn the Japanese bombing of Shanghai and other Chinese cities but that was to be the end of it. He thought it highly unlikely that the United States could be persuaded to join in any effective action and argued that, without their full support, economic sanctions would be futile. The Americans, he insisted, were deeply involved economically in Japan and would be unlikely to sacrifice valuable trade for a mere principle: "It is always best and safest to count on nothing from the Americans but words." For Chamberlain and for Eden, the rise of Fascism in Europe presented a far more immediate threat: he told the Cabinet that he could not imagine anything more suicidal than to pick a quarrel with Japan at such a moment.

*　*　*

The war between Japan and China was one that neither side could win. Militarily the Japanese were unequivocally the superior: better armed, better disciplined, better led. They won victory after victory, each time convinced that *this* would be the decisive moment, that the Chinese would now finally recognise that they could not compete with their invaders and must sue for peace. When Nanking fell to the Japanese in December 1937 joyful crowds celebrated final victory in the streets of Tokyo. But the victory was not final, the Chinese proved obstinately reluctant to admit defeat. No one man can be given exclusive credit – it was the Chinese people whose courage and determination saved the day – but without a leader as inspirational as Chiang Kai-shek it is hard to believe that they would have survived the battering to which they were subjected. Japan's almost complete control of the air meant that China's cities were subjected to a protracted and ruthless bombardment which made the horrors of Guernica seem relatively trivial. Peking was for some reason spared but Tientsin, Hankow, Canton, fell victim to ferocious attacks. Once the Japanese bombers overreached themselves, when they accidentally sank an American gunboat on the Yangtze river. They might reasonably have asked what the gunboat thought it was doing in such a volatile area but instead opted for discretion, apologised and paid substantial damages.

And then the Sino-Japanese war was subsumed into a mightier conflict. What would have happened if there had been no attack on Pearl Harbor, if Japan had not become embroiled with the West? Would Chinese morale finally have cracked or would the Japanese have in the end despaired and withdrawn their forces from the mainland, or at least to Manchuria? As it was, the Japanese achieved astonishing successes against the West, overran South-East Asia, threatened India. If instead they had continued to concentrate their full resources on mainland China it seems almost inconceivable that the Chinese could have continued to resist. And yet they too had almost limitless resources and had shown dauntless determination. At the least the war would have dragged on for years, millions more would have died, an already hideously battered country would have been still further ravaged.

From the point of view of the West the last few months of Japanese activity in China proved to be relatively harmless, almost benign. More and more the chief target of the Japanese became the Chinese Communists; Chiang Kai-shek's forces, without actually accepting the Japanese as allies, at least refrained whenever possible from engaging them in battle. If the Japanese were disarmed, warned the commander of the United States forces, General Wedemeyer, the Communists would move in, take over the Japanese supplies and weapons and assert their supremacy over vast areas of China. It was a curious and ironic twist of circumstances that turned the hated invader into a valued ally in the preservation of liberty against the threat of another and still more dangerous totalitarian power. In one province a group of Japanese was even invited to set up a military academy for the training of Chinese officers.

Such a case was exceptional. The Japanese occupation of China had been too brutal, there had been too many executions, too many rapes, too much wanton destruction for the war to end in anything except bitter hatred. The animosity survives today, though mercifully war between the two powers seems a remote contingency. Perhaps it is desirable that the wounds should never wholly heal, that the memory of that dreadful war should linger in people's minds. Hiroshima, Nagasaki, those are the names that reverberate most immediately in the Japanese consciousness today, but the scars of the long war with China can be little less painful. May they continue to be a reminder of the mistakes that were made in the past and a guarantee that no such mistakes will be made in the future.

NOTES FOR FURTHER READING

There is a plethora of books dealing primarily with the Sino-Japanese war. The most recent is Rana Mitter's *China's War with Japan 1937–1945* (London 2013). An earlier but valuable account is that by John Hunter Boyle, *China and Japan at War 1937–1955* (Stanford 1972). Bradford A. Lee's *Britain and the Sino-Japanese War 1937–1939* (Stanford 1967), as the title suggests, concentrates on the British response to and involvement in the protracted conflict.

19

PALESTINE

1938

On 6 July, 1938, a bomb, presumably planted by a Jewish terrorist, exploded in Haifa, principal port of Palestine. It killed thirty-nine Arabs. The victims could as well have been Jews, killed by an Arab bomb, or British soldiers, who were liable to be attacked by either side. Palestine at the end of the 1930s was a bloody place.

* * *

It all began, perhaps, two thousand years before, but, more immediately, in 1917, when the Balfour Declaration proposed the establishment of a Jewish National Home in Palestine. That the Jews deserved a national home – though many of those who demanded it most vociferously had no intention of going to live there – would today be accepted by most people; that that national home should be located in an area where there was already a large and well-established Arab population was more controversial. The League of Nations made Britain responsible for administering this operation. It proved to be a singularly uncomfortable responsibility. The Arabs bitterly resented their displacement from what they saw as their homeland to make way for an alien invader; the Jews, for their part, felt that the British

British military police searching an Orthodox Jew in Jerusalem, 1938.

were slow to protect their interests, particularly so far as the Holy Places around Jerusalem were concerned.

When the first serious rioting occurred in Palestine, there were some 150,000 Jews already in residence, most of whom were recent immigrants. The Arabs were six times as numerous and the great majority had been born there. As the Jewish population built up, particularly when the trickle of refugees from Nazi Germany became a flood, the Arabs felt that they were under threat. Peaceful co-existence was still possible, but became increasingly difficult. The Jews, for the most part, were more acquisitive, more efficient and often had money to spare; they secured much of the best land, made better use of it than had been the case under the previous owners, and treated Arab interests with an indifference that was at the best tactless, at the worst provocative. The Arabs were duly provoked. The British-controlled government, claimed an Arab newspaper, was "deliberately flooding the country with Jews with the effect of displacing Arabs from the land and depriving them of employment". Illegal immigration, it was claimed, was not merely being condoned, it was being actively encouraged. A general strike was called in protest; angry crowds demonstrated in Jaffa, Nablus, Haifa and Jerusalem, police were stoned, eighteen of the Arab leaders were arrested, accused of inciting disorder and only released on a promise that they would keep the peace for three years at least. Moderates on both sides suffered the usual fate of moderates; they were denounced as cowards or traitors.

"The Jews are so clever and the Arabs so stupid and childish," observed a young British officer, "that it seems only sporting to be for the Arabs." Time and again the Arabs were outwitted, outmanoeuvred and outspent. The problem from their point of view was that what Britain and France had intended to become no more than a Jewish homeland, a place of refuge for the Jews dislodged from Europe, swiftly developed into a Jewish state, a political unit in which anyone who was not Jewish could be only a second-class citizen. If one man was above all responsible for this process it was the Zionist leader, Chaim Weizmann. For Weizmann there was "one fundamental fact – that we must have Palestine if we are not going to be exterminated". Born in Russia, educated in Germany and Switzerland, lecturer in chemistry in Manchester: from the first moment at which he became politically conscious Weizmann knew that his spiritual home must be Jerusalem. It became the principal object of his life to ensure that this spiritual home should be also his domestic and political home. To achieve this he needed the support, or at least the acquiescence, of the British. From the moment in 1918 at which he led the first Jewish delegation to the Zionist Commission for Palestine he made this his primary concern,

On his first visit there he disliked Jerusalem intensely. "It's such an accursed city, there's nothing there, no creature comforts," he wrote disparagingly. But this only fortified his resolve to establish it as the Jewish capital and thus give it the moral – if not yet the physical – grandeur that must go with such a role. He pleaded with the British Foreign Secretary, Arthur Balfour, that he should be allowed to establish a Hebrew University. The British deprecated the creation of any institution that would cater exclusively for Jews but were reluctant to intervene too vigorously in the matter. The Jews had their way. The British were similarily thwarted when they tried to establish an elite public school – based on the British model – where the cream of Palestine's youth, Arab as well as Jewish, would study, at first in Arabic and Hebrew, later in English. "Here was an opportunity of bringing Jews and Arabs together on common ground," wrote the Director of Education. The opportunity was lost: "The Jewish national home needed Jewish national education," concluded a senior Zionist official. In both these cases it was the Jews who were determined to preserve the barriers between Jews and Arabs. Left to themselves, the Arabs would not have greeted the concept of a Jewish–Arab school or university with any great enthusiasm but they would have been unlikely to have prevented their establishment or even to have discouraged young Arabs from attending them.

What was true of the schools and universities applied equally to every other institution and, ultimately, to the land itself. The Arabs, though with regrets, accepted that they must be prepared to share what they regarded as their homeland and to tolerate the concept of co-existence with the Jews. The Jews, though they hesitated overtly to espouse ethnic cleansing, in effect adopted that principle. They knew that they could not forcibly eject *all* the Arabs from Palestine – apart from anything else they needed them to provide an agricultural labour force – but they worked towards that end, denying Arabs equal opportunities, buying up their land, encouraging emigration. The partition of Palestine – its division into two distinct Arab and Jewish parts – had at one time been the favoured solution of the British. The Arabs rejected it because it would inevitably have involved the expulsion of many of them from land where they had lived for many years, sometimes several centuries. The Jews were more enthusiastic: at least it would ensure the essential principle of a Jewish nation state and, as to the frontiers, there was no assurance that they would not be rectified over the years to Israel's advantage. Then the British abandoned the idea as being too complicated, too expensive, too difficult to impose and administer. David Ben-Gurion, Israel's first Prime Minister, later claimed that, if partition had been carried out and a Jewish homeland established in the 1930s, millions of Jews who perished in the holocaust would have found a refuge in their new national home. The claim is questionable: even if they had had the means of getting there the diminished area of Jewish Palestine could not have accommodated so many refugees. It was a missed opportunity, nevertheless: partition would perhaps have created as many problems as it solved but many deaths might not have come about and much misery and destruction might have been averted. The idea of partition was not finally and formally abandoned until the holding of the London Conference on the future of Palestine in March 1939 but it had been accepted that the cause was lost months if not years before.

* * *

From that moment it was just a question of how soon inter-racial tension would degenerate into widespread violence. The Arabs – perhaps because they were the more put-upon – were the prime offenders. The country was being flooded with Jewish immigrants, they complained, many of them legal, more still illegal but tacitly condoned by the authorities. As early as the end of 1933 the Arab Executive was calling a general strike and organising demonstrations in the streets of Jerusalem, Haifa and Jaffa. Such protests were brought under control without too much difficulty, but Arab fears were undiminished. The rise of Fascism in Germany and Italy, with its virulent anti-Semitism and inevitable collision with British and French interests in the Middle East, both vastly increased the exodus of Jews from Europe and gave the Arabs potential allies, who might not have either the inclination or the resources to intervene effectively in the area but were nevertheless delighted to foment opposition to the established powers. Arab terrorism grew, directed primarily against the Jews but including among its targets any non-Arab elements that seemed to threaten its supremacy. Inevitably, there grew up a community of interests between the British and the Jews. In 1933 or 1934 the British authorities would have considered both Jews and Arabs as likely enemies, to be treated with suspicion if not hostility; by 1938, though they still tried to deal even-handedly with both sides, they viewed the Arabs as the principal threat and the Jews as neutral, even as potential allies. Though the officers of the Palestinian police force – which itself was close to being a paramilitary organisation – were predominantly British, most of the rank-and-file were Arab. Several thousand Jews were now enrolled. Nominally they were servants of the British; in fact their loyalties were primarily to the Jewish Agency for Palestine, which had been formally created in 1929 and was recognised by the British as the representative body of the Jews under the Mandate. "You must follow all orders you receive from the government," the future Prime Minister, Moshe Shertok, told them, "but you have another moral obligation . . . to accept not only the government's discipline , but also that of the Jewish leadership." It was hardly necessary to point out where their loyalties should lie if it so happened that the views of the British government and the Jewish leadership were radically different.

As a war in Europe seemed more inevitable and the plight of the Jews became ever more desperate, it might have been expected that Britain and France would become more sympathetic towards Jewish aspirations in the Middle East. The contrary proved true. The problem, from the point of view of the Jews, was that their commitment to the West was *too* unequivocal, there could be no doubt about their total devotion to the Allied cause, they had nowhere else to go. The Arabs, on the other hand, felt no such commitment: it was therefore important for the British to do nothing that might encourage them to do some sort of deal with the Axis powers. The only trump card that the Jews held was their supposed influence in the making of American foreign policy; but since that influence could hardly be used except to try to urge the United States into war with Germany, it did not seem that this need be a matter of great concern to the British. Neville Chamberlain, Britain's Prime Minister when the war broke out, was more pro-Arab than most of his colleagues, but on the whole "a plague on both your houses" was the British attitude. "I think them each as loathsome as the other," declared the British Ambassador to Egypt with improper, though in its way splendidly undiplomatic honesty. "There is only one people on earth that I am thoroughly 'pro' and that's the British!"

The fact that the British were genuinely uncommitted and

saw – and even up to a point sympathised with – the points of view of the two parties, inevitably ensured that they would be disliked and distrusted by both. They could not escape from their responsibilities – under the terms of the Mandate they were doomed to govern Israel until some stable and permanent settlement was achieved – but increasingly had to play their part in the face of active opposition. From the point of view of both Jew and Arab they were, however, a secondary target. The British genuinely wanted to go, both Jew and Arab conceded, in the end they would go, and when they did go the battlefield would be left clear for the two parties who belonged to Palestine and who felt that Palestine belonged to them.

It was a battle that had long been raging: sometimes fierce, sometimes desultory. The atrocity described in the opening paragraph of this essay was only one of a melancholy series of such incidents. As early as April 1936 the Zionist Vladimir Zhabotinsky was recording "alarming reports from Palestine voicing acutest apprehension of anti-Jewish outbreaks". The outbreaks duly followed. Ten days later two Jews were taken off a bus in the Nablus mountains and murdered by a group of armed Arabs; only two days after that two Arabs were killed by Jewish terrorists, members of a body that was to achieve semi-mythic status as the Irgun Zvai Leumi. On both sides there were men of moderation who deplored the worst excesses. Shlomo Ben-Yosef was a Jewish terrorist who was responsible for an attack on an Arab bus in April 1938. He was arrested, tried and executed. A black flag was hung over the Jewish headquarters. David Ben-Gurion, the most eminent Jewish figure in Palestine, ordered that it should be removed. "I am not shocked that a Jew was hanged in

Palestine," he declared. " I am ashamed of the deed that led to the hanging." But for every Ben-Gurion there were two fanatics and it was fanaticism that fired Jewish and Arab youth and in the end forced the would-be moderates into acceding to their demands for violence.

The British, desperate to extricate themselves from this imbroglio and genuinely anxious to find some solution which would allow Palestine to achieve something approaching democracy, now proposed to establish a legislative council, in which Jews and Arabs could jointly undertake the government of their country. The Arabs, conscious of the fact that they would command a majority in any such body, favoured, or at least did not oppose, the idea. The Jews, for the same reason, opposed it. They could not agree, they contended, to the establishment of any body that was overtly hostile to the concept of a Jewish homeland. Such an institution would be "a source of friction and antagonism between the two sections of the population of Palestine, and would destroy the hopes of common united co-operation between the population and the government." Such hopes, if they still existed at all, were frail indeed by the time that the Nineteenth Zionist Congress rejected the idea of a council. Violence became ever more rife: each party, acting, as it saw it, in self-defence, built up its forces so as to protect itself from the threats of its enemy.

The British tried to confine their role to the protection and maintenance of essential services; they built up their military presence in Palestine but sought wherever possible to avoid confrontation with local militias, whether Jewish or Arab. Increasingly such confrontation was thrust upon them. In the second half of 1937 and in 1938 they made genuine attempts to limit Jewish immigration, but their efforts, largely unavailing, merely annoyed the Jews without allaying the fears of the Arabs. When the comparatively liberal and open-minded Weizmann was replaced as Jewish leader by the more truculent Ben-Gurion, the Jewish attitude hardened still further. Both men had given evidence to the Royal Commission, headed by Lord Peel, which the British government sent to Palestine at the end of 1936: Weizmann was the more eloquent and the more emollient but it was Ben-Gurion who stated the Jewish case with the greater passion and authority: "I say on behalf of the Jews that the Bible is our Mandate, the Bible which was written by us, in our own language, in Hebrew, in this very country." It was Ben-Gurion's doctrine that prevailed and the Arab revolt that broke out towards the end of 1937 was largely fuelled by their conviction that the Jewish case was gaining ground and that only violent action could prevent the *de facto* if not *de jure* transformation of Palestine into a Jewish homeland.

1938 was marked by a series of atrocities, not many aimed directly against the British but all calculated to make civil government impossible. The British reacted with ferocity. The High Commissioner, Harold MacMichael, who took office in February 1938, was a colonial civil servant and an Arab speaker who might have been expected to view the Zionists with suspicion if not dislike. On the whole he fulfilled that expectation, but he showed no corresponding sympathy with the Arab cause. His duty, as he saw it, was first and foremost to maintain the peace: since at that time it was the Arabs who presented the greatest threat to that peace, it was the Arabs who were his principal target. "If we must offend one side," Neville Chamberlain was recorded as saying in Cabinet, "let us offend the Jews rather than the Arabs." Other things being equal, that would have been McMichael's guiding principle. But other things were not equal. By a combination of bad luck, ineptness on the part of the Arabs and skilful manoeuvring on the part of the Jews, it was the Arabs who presented themselves most forcibly as seeking to disrupt the established order, the Jews who seemed content to maintain it. When, in June 1938, the British hanged a Jewish youth who had shot at an Arab bus, the Irgun Zvai Leumi retaliated, not directly against the British, but by a series of attacks on the Arab population. One of the most conspicuous of these was the atrocity described in the opening paragraph of this chapter. The bomb was placed in the fruit market at Haifa, timed to explode when things were likely to be at their busiest. Something very similar had happened a few weeks before, killing eighteen Arabs and five Jews: this attack was deadlier. About forty Arabs died and another sixty or so were injured (estimates of the casualties vary widely: some put the death roll far higher but most agree that between forty and fifty people were killed, the great majority of whom were Arab). Even this was by no means the worst of the atrocities, which continued until the summer of 1939, but it was the most widely reported and, at the time, seemed uniquely horrible. The Palestine conflict was not finally resolved until the termination of the British mandate and the creation of independent Israel in May 1948. Some, indeed, would say that it has not finally been resolved even today. But the murders in Haifa on 6 July, 1938, in their total pointlessness and in the indifference shown by their perpetrators to the guilt or innocence of those involved, seem to encapsulate all that was most regrettable about that bitter and protracted conflict.

NOTES FOR FURTHER READING

A library of books has been written about the Arab-Israeli conflict and the birth of Israel. Four which I found particularly valuable from their different points of view were Volume 2 of *Palestine. A Study of Jewish, Arab and British Policies* (Yale 1947), N. A. Rose's *The Gentile Zionists* (London 1973), Conor Cruse O'Brien's opinionated but exceptionally readable *The Siege. The Saga of Israel and Zionism* (London 1986) and Tom Segev's *One Palestine Complete* (London 2000).

20

THE FASCISTS TAKE MADRID

1939

On 28 March, 1939, despite dogged resistance throughout a siege lasting two and a half years, a Fascist army under General Eugenio Espinosa occupied Madrid. Though here and there pockets of resistance still remained, effectively the Civil War was over.

* * *

The Spanish Civil War, Antony Beevor has remarked, is perhaps the best example of a subject which becomes more confusing when it is simplified. Nowhere is this more true than in its origins. In one, perhaps its simplest form, it was a battle of right against left, of the capitalist against the proletariat, of the haves against the have-nots. Viewed from another angle it was a war that pitted the authoritarian against the liberal; a conflict between those who instinctively opposed change just because it *was* change and those who welcomed it for the same reason. Finally it was a war between the centralist and the regionalist, between a government in Madrid that felt Spain should be run as an ever more coherent and cohesive unit, and the fringe communities, in particular the Basques and the Catalans, who craved, if not full independence, then at least something close to political and economic autonomy.

General Francisco Franco, arm outstretched, salutes troops in his Madrid
victory parade in May 1939.

Similar conflicts of interest, in varying forms and strengths, were also to be found in France and Britain; Spain was not unique in falling prey to forces that seemed to defy reconciliation. Somehow, however, in France and Britain, compromises were found, issues fudged, slowly and sometimes painfully a consensus evolved. The condition of Spain today shows that such a resolution of its problems would not always prove impossible to attain. In 1936, however, the fissiparous tendencies were too strong, the price to be paid for compromise seemed too high. It took three years of vicious war and thirty-one years of dictatorship to convince the Spanish people that there was another way.

No one individual can be held responsible for steering Spain on to the course that ended in civil war but if the army had not found in General Franco a man who was not only ready to accept supreme power but also able to exercise it with skill and ruthless determination it is possible that the nation might have muddled through to something close to true democracy. Franco was far from being the principal instigator of the military coup of July 1936, but from the moment at which he and his African troops moved to the mainland from Spanish Morocco it became evident that he was the leading figure in the revolutionary forces and that, if those forces finally prevailed, it was he who would assume supreme power.

"Power tends to corrupt, and absolute power corrupts absolutely." Lord Acton's adage was never more true than when applied to Franco. All the indications are that, when he was first charged with supreme military command and then created head of government, he envisaged a future in which some degree of democratic rule would eventually be restored and his own authority, if not altogether waived, would be exercised with due restraint. This could not come about at once, however. Franco had good reason to believe that Spain not only needed but, for the most part, actually craved strong government. He provided it and, in so doing, was himself seduced by power. Legitimate opposition began to seem to him to be irresponsible, even treasonable. In a Europe in which Hitler's Germany and Mussolini's Italy seemed the most successful and dynamic countries, it was inevitable that Franco's Spain should emulate their achievements and range itself with the Fascist powers.

But Spain did not become "Franco's Spain" without a long and painful conflict. The "Nationalists", as the followers of Franco were generally known, established themselves firmly in the south and east but failed to take control of several of the largest cities: Barcelona, Valencia, Málaga and, most notably, Madrid. Left to themselves the Spaniards might possibly have run out of steam and ended the conflict quickly, but outside powers elected to interfere and fight a war by proxy on Spanish soil. The Germans and Italians threw their weight behind the Nationalists, the Russians supported the Republicans. France and Great Britain were generally sympathetic to the Republicans and many French and British citizens went to war on that side, but, their governments' official line being one of non-intervention, they fought as individuals.

The war was waged with pitiless ferocity. Though the Republicans fought bravely and with determination, the Nationalists were better disciplined and better armed. By October 1936 they had reached the outskirts of Madrid but, though the Republican government thought it necessary to flee the city and install itself in Valencia, its troops, bolstered by the support of some three thousand volunteers from the International Brigade, succeeded in keeping the attackers at bay. "It is better to die on your feet than to live on your knees," cried Dolores Ibárruri, *La Pasionaria*, the passionate young idol of the Spanish Communists. But neither in Madrid nor in Valencia were the Republicans united; the army in due course turned out the ruling government and installed a National Defence Council. This in its turn split: the Communist elements attacking the ruling junta, who were disposed to do a deal with the rampant Nationalists. The Communists were defeated, but when the Republicans tried to negotiate a settlement it became clear that the Nationalists were not disposed to accept any terms short of unconditional surrender. No compromise was possible. Franco was obsessed by his desire to take the capital but his councillors prevailed on him first to concentrate on the more strategically important regions to the north and east. The international press, who agreed with Franco that Madrid must be the target of any offensive conducted on rational lines, found it hard to comprehend that this switch in emphasis had taken place. Hubert Knickerbocker, one of the most celebrated of foreign correspondents, actually reported the fall of the city and described in vivid terms the march of the triumphant Nationalist troops into the city. He was not as wrong as all that – at one point Moorish troops had fought their way to within a few hundred yards of the city centre – but the offensive was contained. For the moment Madrid survived: yet so dire was the plight of its defenders that some of them must occasionally have wondered whether it would not have been better if they had lost the battle and the city had fallen to Franco's armies.

* * *

Alhough the vast majority of the people of Madrid were united in their determination to fight and, if necessary, die in defence of their city, there were some who saw things differently. When the Commander of the Nationalist Army of the North, Emilio Mola, was asked which of the four columns poised to attack the city was likely to be the first to reach its objective, he replied that it would be none of them but a fifth column of Nationalist supporters who were lurking within the city ready to rise and stab the defenders in the back when the right moment came. This was the first use of the phrase "fifth column", a concept that was to spread much terror in the forthcoming Second World War. In fact, in this case, it had little reality: though many of its inhabitants fled Madrid, those who remained were astonishing in their courage and resolution.

The end of 1936 saw an ugly lull. Madrid was under siege, but though the encircling enemy were able to prevent supplies of any substance reaching the city, the blockade was never so tight that individuals were unable to slip in and out more or less as they pleased.

There was only a relatively small chance that any individual would be killed in Madrid in 1937 and 1938 but it was still a thoroughly unpleasant place in which to live. Because of its greater size the city did not suffer the virtual obliteration that had been the fate of Guernica, but the aerial bombardment was far more persistent. In what may have been a deliberate attempt to foment dissension within the city, the affluent suburbs in the Salamanca district were spared, but all other residential areas were heavily attacked. "I will destroy Madrid rather than leave it to the Marxists!" declared Franco; the fact that, in so doing, he destroyed the property of many of his own followers, including the palace of the Duke of Alba, was no doubt regretted but was deemed of inconsiderable importance in the wider pattern of the war. German Junkers Ju-52 bombers were prominent in the attack from the air. The German chargé d'affaires, alarmed at the damage that was being done to his country's reputation, pleaded that "as long as Lufthansa traffic continues, no Junkers raid Madrid". No attention was paid to his pleas: the following day the Junkers landed four bombs on the War Ministry. Protest meetings were held outside the German Embassy and the chargé urged that he and his staff should be withdrawn. Again he was ignored: he would have been still more put out if he had known that German military advisers were urging Franco to step up the bombardment and blast the recalcitrant inhabitants of Madrid into submission.

The diplomats were not the only foreigners to witness Madrid's travail at first hand. The Spanish Civil War was reported in vivid detail in all the leading newspapers of the world. The attention paid to these accounts was in part explained by the remarkable quality of the coverage. The war was witnessed by some of the greatest writers of the age, among them Ernest Hemingway, George Orwell, W. H. Auden, André Malraux, John Dos Passos, Stephen Spender, Simone Weil. Most of them took the side of the Republic though some, like Evelyn Waugh and Ezra Pound, openly supported Franco, and others, like Spender, were horrified by the excesses of which the Republicans were guilty and lost all enthusiasm for the conflict. By the time the siege was nearing its end almost all of them had left. One of the few who stayed until the fall of the city was O'Dowd Gallagher of the *Daily Express*, "A hard-drinking, half-Irish, half-South African," as Paul Preston describes him. Like most of his colleagues Gallagher assumed that he would witness a savage house-by-house defence of the city; instead he was surprised to find that, when the siege finally came to an end, almost the only people to be seen in the streets were, or appeared to be, Nationalist supporters. The "fifth column" emerged from the cellars to cheer the Fascist liberators; the great mass of the population remained discreetly indoors and tried to look as if it had played no part in the conflict.

The end had come with disconcerting rapidity. In the last four weeks of Madrid's existence as a Republican city the preoccupation of the defenders had been more the power struggle within their own ranks than with the increasingly inevitable advent of the Nationalists. It was a struggle that was won emphatically by the Left, who enjoyed a brief and illusory glimpse of power. The probability of their imminent extinction made the hitherto unscaleable barriers between the Anarchists and the Socialists appear suddenly of slight importance; even the few traces of capitalism that survived seemed, if not to be applauded, then at least not something that required urgent correction. A single command was established, the city in its entirety was mobilised. Madrid in its dying hours achieved a unity that had eluded it in happier times.

Gratifying though this no doubt was to those involved, it could not affect the outcome of the war. On November 6, the leader of the ruling coalition, Francisco Largo Caballero, announced that he was abandoning the city and moving the seat of government to Valencia. The President, Manuel Azaña, had already fled, without even telling his ministers that that was his intention. It was an ignominious scuttle, with only a handful of anarchist ministers arguing that it would be better to stay, fight and, in all probability, die in defence of the capital. Two passenger aircraft were earmarked for the transport of the refugees but nobody made use of them. The ministers left by road and passed through what should have been enemy lines with disconcerting ease. The only trouble came when anarchist militiamen turned on a group of refugees, including the Foreign Minister, and drove them back towards the city.

They found themselves almost alone when they got there. Madrid, official Madrid at least, was left deserted. Mikhail Kol'tsov, *Pravda*'s leading foreign correspondent and an ardent advocate of continued resistance, made his way to the War Ministry. "I climbed the stairs to the lobby. Not a soul! On the landing . . . two old employees are seated, like wax figures, wearing livery and neatly shaven, waiting to be called by the Minister . . . Rows of offices! All the doors are wide open . . . The ceiling lamps shine brightly. On the desks there are abandoned maps, documents, communiqués, pencils, pads filled with notes. Not a soul!" General José Miaja, a veteran who had made a mess of an attack on Cordoba and had been shunted into honourable retirement, found himself resurrected and nominated President of the National Defence Council. It was an honour which he would willingly have foregone; a chalice, not so much empty, as containing only a few unappealing dregs. His charge was to defend Madrid "at all costs". Any convincing defence, it was obvious, was beyond his powers; the cost of trying to provide it was likely to be extravagantly high.

The units on which he could depend with the greatest confidence – both for their discipline and their readiness to fight – were those manned by members of the Communist Party. This can hardly have increased his optimism about the long-term future. The Communists' first priority was undoubtedly to defend the city against Fascist incursions but they made no bones about the fact that they intended to ensure that it was a Communist Madrid that survived once the siege was over. For the time being they would offer some sort of co-operation with anyone who could provide effective resistance to the common enemy but they missed no opportunity to infiltrate all the positions of power and to sideline or even murder those whom they saw as an obstacle to their long-term ambitions. The Madrid which the Nationalists occupied in March 1939 was to all intents and purposes a Communist city, or at least a city in which the non-Communist members of society found it expedient to remain discreetly under cover.

With the Nationalists at the gates of the city, it was obvious to its inhabitants, whatever their political inclinations, that the war was lost. In fact the Republicans still controlled nearly a third of Spanish territory and they had half a million men under arms, but they were short of weapons and ammunition, many of the most belligerent leaders were dead, those who were left were demoralised and not disposed to battle on to the bitter end. In Madrid the civilian population, what was left of it, was in a desperate plight. There was barely enough food to keep it alive, malnutrition was rife, what small supplies that remained were being rapidly exhausted and it seemed more and more uncertain whether they could be replenished. Heating was a luxury available only to a privileged few, water was in short supply and had to be severely rationed. Medical supplies, even the most basic bandages and antiseptics, had almost disappeared and the doctors and surgeons – many of whom had disappeared as well – had to make do with whatever inadequate substitutes they could conjure up. Even if the Republicans had had the stomach to continue the fight they would have found it almost impossible to do so; as it was, Franco's army arrived at the outskirts of Madrid expecting to have to fight its way, street by street, house by house, into the centre and instead found what was virtually an open city. Many of the inhabitants remained prudently within their houses while the way was lined by cheering citizens, who either genuinely welcomed the advent of the Fascists or felt it wise to appear to do so. "*Han Pasado!*" they called triumphantly; a mocking echo of *La Pasionaria's* proud words of two years before. "After a two-and-a-half-year siege," reported O'Dowd Gallagher, "[Madrid] surrendered today and tonight is completely under General Franco's control."

* * *

Spain would not have been Spain and civil war not civil war if the Nationalist victory had not been followed by a certain amount of bloodletting. There were many murders or summary executions, many show trials in which the guilt of the defendants was taken for granted from the start. But, viewed in the light of the horrors of the Spanish Civil War itself, the aftermath was relatively muted. It was as if the bloodlust had at last been sated; the people had been sickened by the horrors of the war and wanted only to put it behind them and, so far as possible, forget it. "So far as possible" is, however, a significant qualification. Even after the first wave of more or less random executions, many thousands of those who had fought on the losing side or were even suspected of sympathising with the Republican cause were penned up and treated with striking harshness. The concentration camps which were to become so prominent and painful a feature of Axis-dominated Europe found their progenitors in Franco's Spain. Nearly half a million Republicans, or people whom it suited the Francoists to treat as Republicans, were from time to time cooped up in these cages; more than a hundred camps remained open in the 1940s, the last one did not close until 1947. Count Ciano, the Italian Foreign Minsiter, who was well disposed towards the regime, reported that, as late as July 1939 there were "trials going on every day at a speed that I would almost call summary . . . There are still a great number of shootings. In Madrid alone between 200 and 250 a day . . ."

Things would probably have been no better if the other side had won. It is in the nature of civil wars that they are fought with striking bitterness and leave most painful scars behind. Of none is this more true that the Spanish Civil War. For all their abilities and great achievements the Spanish have seldom been noted for their moderation. Never was this more apparent than in the years that followed the flight of the dictator, General Miguel Primo de Rivera, and the collapse of the monarchy in 1931, which had ushered in the second republic. Espinosa's entry into Madrid, marking as it did the virtual end of eight years' ferocious anarchy and bloodshed, to some seemed a reason for rejoicing, to others anguish, but there can have been few who were not conscious of feeling a certain relief.

NOTES FOR FURTHER READING

There is an immense body of literature concerning the Civil War. Three of the most comprehensive, balanced and readable books are Hugh Thomas's *The Spanish Civil War* (London 1961), Raymond Carr's *The Spanish Tragedy* (London 1977) and Antony Beevor's *The Spanish Civil War* (London 1982). Paul Preston's *We Saw Spain Die* (London 2008) concentrates on the role of the foreign correspondents. Ernest Hemingway's novel *For Whom the Bell Tolls* (London 1940) provides a moving and disturbing account of this peculiarly ferocious war.

21

DECLARATION OF WAR

1939

I can remember to within a few inches where I was standing at 11.15 on the morning of Sunday 3 September, 1939. It was on the terrace of my parents' house in the New Forest, just outside the French windows that led into the drawing room. From the brown Bakelite box that housed our recently acquired wireless came the melancholy, slightly bleating voice of the Prime Minister, Neville Chamberlain. No reply, he said, had been received to the ultimatum that we and the French had delivered to Nazi Germany, demanding that their troops must immediately withdraw from Polish territory: "Consequently this country is at war with Germany." I thought the turn of events was rather exciting: war promised to be something of an adventure, much more interesting than the humdrum existence that I had so far led. I noticed that my father, who had fought in Mesopotamia and on the Western Front in the First World War, seemed rather discomposed by the news. I wondered why.

* * *

It could have come much earlier. The more prescient had accepted that eventual war was a probability if not a certainty as soon as the Nazis took power in Germany. The only question

Big Ben strikes eleven on Sunday September 3, 1939.
The Second World War has begun.

was how long it could be delayed. The *Anschluss*, Germany's armed takeover of Austria in March 1938, marked a further stage in the march to Armageddon. Still, the more naïve or more optimistic continued to believe that Hitler's appetite would be satisfied by this new acquisition. There was little talk of economic sanctions, none of military intervention. "England has sent me a protest," Hitler observed. "I would have understood a declaration of war; to a protest I shall not even reply." The British and French governments would have argued that, even if the people had had the will to fight, they lacked the means. Rearmament was only just getting under way; even if Austria had invited the West to come to its assistance there would have been no forces available with which to make an effective intervention. To this the response is that Germany was little better prepared – the balance of power in September 1939 was not significantly different to what it had been eighteen months before. Rightly or wrongly, anyway, the West concluded that there was no case for doing more than make disapproving noises. Hitler licked his lips, bided his time and made plans for his next exercise in aggrandisement.

It was not long in coming. Czechoslovakia was the most tempting target. The country had been created more or less arbitrarily after the First World War. Its most heavily industrialised province, Sudetenland, contained a substantial German population which considered itself – not wholly without justification – to be an underprivileged and misused minority. The Western leaders, Neville Chamberlain being most prominent among them, believed that the Sudeten Germans had a case and that there should be territorial adjustments. This, Chamberlain believed, or at least professed to believe, would be the end of it: the seizure of the whole of Czechoslovakia, he assured his sister, Ida, "would not be in accordance with Herr Hitler's policy, which is to include all Germans in the Reich but not to include other nationalities". Acting under this delusion, the British urged the Czechs to make substantial territorial concessions: "The general feeling," that champion of confrontation, Duff Cooper, remarked, "seemed to be that great, brutal Czechoslovakia was bullying poor, peaceful little Germany!"

To add to the woes of Czechoslovakia, the territories that were to be transferred to Germany contained almost all the frontier fortifications on which they depended to defend themselves. Before September they would have found it difficult to mount any convincing defence against a German invasion; after September it became impossible. Chamberlain, whose energy in the pursuit of peace was as admirable as his policies proved to be disastrous, returned in triumph from the negotiations in Munich to be greeted by cheering crowds. "You might think that we'd won a major victory," observed a Foreign Office official sourly, "instead of just betraying a minor country."

Chamberlain genuinely believed that he could trust Hitler and that he had secured, if not necessarily peace in our time, then peace with honour and a peace that could be expected to last at least for a few years. To Churchill it was painfully obvious that what had been achieved was peace with dishonour and, still worse, that no more had been gained than a few months of precarious passivity. The price paid had been too high, the benefit too small. "We seem to be very near the bleak choice between War and Shame," he wrote. "My feeling is that we shall choose

Shame, and then have War thrown in a little later, on even more adverse terms than at present."

It took only a few months for him to be proved dismally correct. Germany had almost a million men under arms, and at that point gave up any pretence of abiding by the recruitment restrictions of the Versailles Treaty and introduced full conscription, a frightening reminder that this already heavily armed nation was far better prepared for war than its more easy-going rivals. The persecution of the Jews was redoubled and Hitler made renewed play with Germany's need for *Lebensraum* (living space), if it was to be able to house and feed its rapidly growing population. At whose expense that living space would be acquired he did not specify, but that it must be towards the east was obvious. When, on April 28, Hitler denounced the Non-Aggression Pact which Germany had signed with Poland five years earlier, it became clear what the next target was destined to be.

Though nothing could condone outright aggression, Hitler had some grounds for discontent over the state of affairs in Poland. The inhabitants of Danzig and the Polish Corridor were predominantly German. They longed to be reunited with their motherland and, though they could not with good reason claim to be seriously misused by their present rulers, they kept up a sustained grumble which found receptive ears in Berlin. The last thing that he wanted, Hitler protested, was to occupy any Polish territory, but he could not ignore the pleas of his fellow countrymen. Two things only deterred him from taking drastic action to remedy their misfortunes. The first was the likely attitude of the French and British. On the whole, he concluded, this was a risk he could afford to run. Their failure to respond effectively to his attack on Czechoslovakia had convinced him that the Western powers were too pacific, too weak, too, as he saw it, cowardly to do more than utter ineffective protests.

The second consideration, the response of Russia, was more questionable. Sooner or later, Hitler was convinced, there would have to be war between Germany and Russia but he was in no hurry to provoke it. Russia was likely to consider a German invasion of Poland a threatening move, and there was a risk that they would feel bound to respond. The easiest way to avoid this was to do a deal and to make the invasion of Poland a joint enterprise, with the country being carved up between the two aggressors. Throughout the summer of 1939 his emissaries in Moscow worked busily to achieve this end. On August 23 they achieved their goal. Within a month German and Russian armies had invaded Poland.

Poland could not long have survived an attack from Germany alone; when subsequently invaded by its vast neighbour to the east, the miracle was that they put up any sort of fight at all. Fifty-six German divisions, including nine armoured units, crossed the border early in the morning on September 1. A few hours later sixteen hundred German bombers began to attack Polish cities, above all, Warsaw. Churchill was the first Englishman to get the news. Count Raczynski, the Polish Ambassador in London, chose to bypass the Foreign Office and Downing Street and go straight to the one man who, he felt sure, would see the need for an instant and emphatic reponse. To Churchill the news came as no surprise; the rest of the British establishment was less well prepared. The reaction of Lord Gort, the Chief of the

Imperial General Staff, was to say that he didn't believe it, the War Office had not been told about it so it could not have happened. When he was finally convinced that Poland was being overrun he ordered full mobilisation but recommended no further action. Nor were the French any more venturesome. Clearly, if Germany refused to withdraw its troops from Poland then Britain and France were bound to go to war, but no-one in London or Paris seems to have believed that this necessarily need lead to any other immediate action.

Whether a golden opportunity was thereby lost is a question that has not been and never will be finally answered. Obviously there was nothing to be done in Poland itself: there was no way by which the Allies could have intervened militarily in a way that would have checked, or even slowed down, the German advance. In the West, though, the situation was different. Anxious to overrun Poland with a minimum of delay and mindful of the possibility that a confrontation with Russia was not inconceivable, Hitler had concentrated his forces in the east and left only ten divisions to defend the French frontier. In theory at least, an all-out offensive might have breached the Siegfried Line and laid Germany open to invasion. In practice it was not so easy. The British Expeditionary Force was still more of a concept than a reality and could have contributed nothing to the enterprise. The French were better prepared but still not poised to strike: neither militarily nor, more important, psychologically, were they in a state to contemplate any sort of full-blooded offensive.

Instead both governments hesitated: Chamberlain assuring the House of Commons that there was still a possibility that Hitler might think better of his projects; the Football Association announcing that the situation did not warrant the cancellation of the next day's matches. Even Churchill, though he was by now convinced that war could not and should not be avoided, hesitated to portray himself as a warmonger. In the debate in the House of Commons on September 2 he chose not to speak.

Though war finally could not be avoided, there were those in the government who felt that it need not amount to much. As Samuel Hoare told the Cabinet, they could "always fulfil the letter of the declaration without going all out". Honour, or at least Chamberlain's conception of honour, would be satisfied if Britain and France fulfilled their obligations by going to war with Germany but then did nothing very much about it. When the dust had settled in Poland it would surely be possible to patch up some sort of compromise – settling tender consciences, perhaps, by persuading Hitler, once he had destroyed the Polish army and dismantled its government, to set up some sort of puppet state which would enjoy a semblance of independence. It was an illusion that Hitler was happy to foster.

For several years Britain had been exposed to images of cities ravaged by bombardment from the air. Guernica, Barcelona, now it was Warsaw. Surely London would be next? The people braced themselves for devastating attacks. They knew that the Royal Air Force and the anti-aircraft batteries would do their best to defend them but they suspected that such efforts would be largely unavailing. "The bomber," as Baldwin had warned, "will always get through." A few moments after war was declared the sirens sounded to announce an enemy attack. "You've got to hand it to Hitler," remarked Churchill, characteristically heading, not for the air-raid shelter, but for the roof of the Admiralty from which he hoped to secure a better view. "The war is less than half an hour old and already he has bombers over London!" Then nothing happened. It was a false alarm triggered off by a stray civilian aircraft. Within a few minutes the All Clear sounded. It was All Clear for the rest of the day, All Clear the next day, All Clear for the weeks and months that followed. Chamberlain's lacklustre words had introduced not a period of heightened drama or noble sacrifice but of inconvenience, irritation and gradually mounting privation. It was the "bore war", the "phoney war". It would not be long before Londoners would look back with nostalgia on that uneasy lull and wish wistfully that it might return, but at the time it seemed an almost intolerable imposition.

NOTES FOR FURTHER READING

The outbreak of the Second World War inevitably figures largely in every history and almost every biography of the period. As valuable as any, if only because it makes one view events through a different perspective, is Albert Speer's *Inside the Third Reich* (London 1970).

EPILOGUE

Twenty-one uneasy years, bounded by two cataclysmic wars: no-one could say that the period between 1919 and 1939 was one of unmarred felicity. The first decade was spent recovering from the First World War; the second preparing for the Second. And yet it did not seem like that at the time. Although, from the moment that the Nazis took power in Germany, the threat of war became ever more evident, the world as a whole rubbed along quite satisfactorily. By 1939 many millions of human beings were better fed, better housed, better dressed, than they had been twenty years before; few were substantially worse off. Happiness is perhaps not to be measured in such terms, yet happiness is more difficult to experience where there is hunger and insecurity. It does not seem extravagant to claim that the world in 1939 was a happier place than it had been in 1919.

It was a period of change which, though dramatic, was at times almost imperceptible. Throughout the nineteenth century, for three millennia indeed, Europe had been the powerhouse of the world. First the Greeks, then the Romans, then the British and French had allowed their insatiable appetite for wealth and power to drive them further and further into imperial adventures. India and China occupied vast hinterlands and China in particular exercised great power outside its frontiers, but they did not seek to establish a worldwide empire; the European nations alone indulged in such extravagance.

But by 1900 a new and virile power was rising in the West: the United States, though it largely limited its physical presence to the American continent, was becoming a force to be reckoned with across the globe. The First World War ravaged Europe, leaving it economically impoverished and bereft of the cream of the generation that should have led it through the coming decades. The New World it hardly touched: the United States at the end of 1918 was immeasurably more significant in terms of global politics that it had been five years before. If it did not necessarily behave as a superpower it was because it had not learnt to think of itself as such: the reality became ever more apparent.

Between the Wars, therefore, deals above all with Europe's recession from power. The final disintegration of Europe's great empires did not take place until after the Second World War; without that war it would certainly have been delayed, perhaps by decades, perhaps even by half a century. But even by 1919 it was inevitable; by 1939, as one can now see, it was inexorably in train. For some this may seem a reason to rejoice, for others to grieve. Whatever one may feel, it happened. The world we live in today was shaped by the events of 1919–1939: it can only enhance our understanding of our present problems and predicaments if we know what our fathers, grandfathers or great-grandfathers experienced eighty or ninety years ago.

INDEX

PICTURE CREDITS:

Page 10: Mary Evans / Everett Collection

Page 34: © London Illustrated News Ltd / Mary Evans

Page 54: Mary Evans / Jeffrey Morgan

Page 70: © London Illustrated News Ltd / Mary Evans

Page 80: Mary Evans Picture Library

Page 94: Robert Sennecke / Ullstein Bild via Getty Images

Page 106: Mary Evans Picture Library

Page 118: Mary Evans / Everett Collection

Page 130: Courtesy Everett Collection / REX / Shutterstock

Page 138: © Photo Researchers / Mary Evans

Page 152: Mary Evans / Sueddeutsche Zeitung Photo

Page 164: Kurt Severin / Ullstein Bild via Getty Images

Page 178: Ullstein Bild via Getty Images

Page 196: © Mary Evans / Glasshouse Images

Page 206: Popperfoto / Getty Images

Page 218: © Danzig Baldaev / FUEL. Reproduced from *Drawings from the Gulag*, page 32. © FUEL Publishing 2010. fuel-design.com

Page 226: © London Illustrated News Ltd / Mary Evans

Page 240: Mary Evans / Everett Collection

Page 254: Mary Evans / Everett Collection

Page 268: Bettmann / Getty Images

Page 282: Mary Evans / Grenville Collins Postcard Collection

Translation of the Russian caption on p.218

One of the instruments of torture that the N.K.V.D. used during interrogations of "enemies of the people" was the rack, which dates back many centuries in Russia.

The "third degree interrogation", legalised by Joseph Stalin and the General Prosecutor of the U.S.S.R., Andrey Vyshinsky, made it possible to obtain any statements from the "enemies of the people" against themselves or others. In order to avoid further torture, many "confessed" to espionage, sabotage, conspiracy, etc, preferring execution by firing squad in the "slaughterhouse" of the U.F.U.* N.K.V.D.

* U.F.U. (Upravlenie Fizicheskogo Unichtozheniya) – the Department of Physical Extermination.

PHILIP ZIEGLER was a diplomat before becoming an editorial director at the publishers William Collins. His many books include acclaimed biographies of Laurence Olivier, William IV, Lady Diana Cooper, Lord Mountbatten and Harold Wilson, as well as the classic history of the Black Death.